THE COCKTAIL

The Rainbow Room, New York City, circa 1950s.

THE
COCKTAIL

*The Influence of Spirits on
the American Psyche*

JOSEPH LANZA

St. Martin's Press
New York

"Cocktails for Two." Words and Music by Arthur Johnston and Sam Coslow. Copyright © 1934 by Famous Music Corporation. Copyright renewed 1961 by Famous Music Corporation. Reprinted with permission.

Design by Junie Lee

Library of Congress Cataloging-in-Publication Data

Lanza, Joseph.
  The cocktail : the influence of spirits on the American psyche / Joseph Lanza.
    p.   cm.
  ISBN 0-312-13450-9
  1. Cocktails—United States—History.   2. Drinking customs—United States.   3. United States—Social life and customs.   I. Title.
  GT2853.U5L35   1995   95-31580
  394.1'3—dc20   CIP

First Edition: November 1995
10 9 8 7 6 5 4 3 2 1

INGREDIENTS

LIST OF ILLUSTRATIONS

ACKNOWLEDGMENTS

THANKS FOR INSPIRATION, ADVICE, AND ASSISTANCE TO:

American Movie Classics
ASCAP
David Baker
Helen Birch
Elizabeth Board
Jamie Brickhouse
Clark Bustard
Jana Christy
Irwin Chusid
Dale DeGroff
DISCUS (Distilled Spirits
    Council of the United
    States)
Jim Fitzgerald
Alison Fraser
Tony Gentry
Regan Good
Evie Greenbaum
Hugh Hardy
Skip Heller
Historical Society of
    Pennsylvania
Tony Holmgrain
Robert Hull
Jonathan Hyams

Jersey City Public Library
Barbara Kafka
Stella Kane
Ken B. Kleman
Mara Lurie
Robyn Massey
Phil Mattera
Francisco Mattos
Barbara McGurn
Elizabeth McNamara
Tina L. Millard
John Mitchell
New York Public Library
    for the Performing Arts
Frank O'Heaney
George Petros
Jon Pope
Richmond-Times
    Dispatch
Van Swearingen
Turner Classic Movies
"Very Vicky" Comics
Marc Weidenbaum
Donna Williams

1

Tipsy Topsy Turvy

Sinatra showed no signs of fatigue during the previous night's [March 5] concert. He sipped from a glass of amber liquid that night, and, in the manner of the late Jackie Gleason, commented on the drink's potency. "Wow!" Sinatra said at one point. "I could light your cigarette with this."

—*Richmond Times-Dispatch,* March 7, 1994

Frank Sinatra almost reached the final curtain the evening of March 6, 1994. During a performance at Virginia's Richmond Mosque Auditorium, he reportedly stopped in the middle of his "My Way" encore, lit a cigarette, fell off a bar stool, and collapsed headfirst in the direction of his fans.

The news reports claimed that Sinatra was "overheated." But numerous accounts of the event have left bits and pieces of unresolved detail. This is especially true when the *Richmond-Times Dispatch* rhapsodized about the singer wielding his trusty "amber" liquid during the previous night's performance, and the *New York Post* reported that he had fallen off of a "vinyl-topped bar stool" the following evening. Since the man and his drink, like the man and his music, are often perceived as matching aesthetics, how could Sinatra truly have it his way with just a bar stool, without the drink to go with it?

For a few moments, the world was in danger of losing an icon that, like an upturned saint, portended apocalypse when knocked from its proper place. Though Sinatra soon recoiled into good health and we were all saved, a mystery remains. What could have passed through Sinatra's mind during his brief flirtation with eternity?

That fragile trajectory by which Sinatra toppled from vertical to horizontal suggests the vectors of a dream by which we may view, through some fourth dimension, a dizzying cavalcade of crystal goblets, swizzle sticks, neon signs, tiki rooms, exotic strip shows, Love Potions, ice cubes, silver shakers, playing cards, poker dice, Martini olives, maraschino cherries, tuxedoed lounge lizards, lush ballroom orchestras, rhumba bands, Catskill comedians, casino crooners and sultry singers, Happy Hour pianos and hotel organs, or whiskey-ridden detectives chasing spies in Shriner fezzes.

These are, after all, the things that make up *the Cocktail,* the aqua vitae that H. L. Mencken once hailed as "the greatest of all the contributions of the American way of life to the salvation of humanity."

The Duchess of Devonshire called it "the world in a glass"; Lord Rothschild believed it "the sweetest form of alchemy"; the modest W. H. Auden settled for it being just "a solace in old age." There have been other such analogies drawn to the car, the airplane, and the skyscraper to symbolize man's achievements, but the cocktail's relevance outshines all of them *precisely* because it seems, at first glance, so trivial.

From the Revolutionary War and the eighteenth-century whiskey rebellions to the curse of Prohibition and the Jazz Age madness, to the Cold War cocktail party, and to today's leisure and entertainment culture, the cocktail continues to serve up proof (80 percent or more) that Western culture can attain a transcendence equal and perhaps superior to that of all other cultures. The cocktail is the ticket to a visionary yet precarious state, when the Gin-and-Tonic tickles the spine, the muscles relax, the lounge piano plays a sentimental tune, and all seems right with the world for at least an hour or two.

Author William Grimes, in his book *Straight Up or On the Rocks,* defines the cocktail as "a glass-enclosed void in which anything can happen, a restless, anxiety-tinged emptiness, forever spinning off variants. The neon martini glass, effulgent symbol of the American bar, is always empty."

Inside that void, however, lurks a prismatic paradise that inspires drinkers and nondrinkers alike: a reentry into Eden via Las Vegas with stopovers in Disneyland. Whether shaken or stirred, sweet or dry, the cocktail is the libation of libertines and mystics alike, spawning as many visions as there are Sinatra songs. So, let's gambol (and at times totter) about with Sinatra and a cast of many other colorful characters on a survey of life through the sublime and distorted lens of a cocktail glass.

2

Is the "Cocktail" as Dirty as It Sounds?

Such a selfish, insolent coxcomb as that, such a cocktail.
—William Makepeace Thackeray,
The Newcomes: Memoirs of a Most Respectable Family

George Washington was a Yankee Doodle dandy who, in petulant rebellion, cocked his star-spangled tail feathers at England and drove King George III even further to insanity. Legend has it that our gun-brandishing Beau Brummel of the Potomac and Founding Father had such an affection for sartorial flash that he inspired a revolutionary toast. One evening during their usual drinking binge, Washington and his fellow officers ran out of toasting topics. Eying the general's feathered cap, one of the soldiers declared: "A toast to the cock's tail!" Hence, the term *cocktail* was born.

This is but one of the many apocryphal anecdotes tracing this ambiguous, titillating, and somewhat risqué expression. Still, there is no incontrovertible evidence as to when or how "cocktail" first appeared. Even once it was widely used, the word continued to evolve into an accretion of metaphors that the brash Americans cherished and the more reserved British regarded with suspicion.

The *Oxford English Dictionary* indicates that "cocktail" originally denoted a hybrid animal, usually a mixed-breed horse passing itself off as a thoroughbred but often distinguished by a bobbed tail. One story claims that the renowned Samuel Johnson had this definition in mind when, on one occasion, his friend Boswell served him wine laced with gin. Taken aback, Johnson called the mixture "a veritable cocktail of a drink." The *OED* also uses "cocktail" to describe a poseur projecting the air of a gentleman but lacking true gentlemanly breeding. A reference in the June 11, 1887, issue of the British journal *The Academy* veers close to defining a lounge lizard when gibing at "cocktails who blunder into liaisons with barmaids." From hybrid breeding to hybrid mores, "cocktail" would inevitably denote hybrid liquors congealing in a genetically reengineered beverage.

The cocktail may seem prefabricated and precious, but it came into the world with guts and gore. Some historians speculate that the Revolutionary War was partly due to Britain's efforts to force the Colonies to buy only British rum at the expense of the French and Spanish markets. Even Paul Revere had to fuel up at the Isaac Hall rum distillery before he could successfully make his famous ride.

In times of relative peace, Washington was also

known to be a proud drinker who once rewarded his constituency by doling out seventy-five gallons of free rum just before he was elected to Virginia's House of Burgesses. Later, the great Whiskey Rebellion of 1794 (and a test for federalism) occurred in Pennsylvania when farmers refused to endure the tax that Washington was now imposing on their distilleries.

The Revolutionary War connection resurfaces with the "Flanagan Fallacy." In 1779, Betsy Flanagan was an innkeeper at a tavern in Westchester County, New York's, Four Corners. A French customer, enamored with his hostess, lifted his glass and shouted: "To Betsy and her marvelous drink! It offers to the palate the same delightful sensations as the cock's tail feathers offer to the eye! Vive le Cocktail!" Other accounts claim that Betsy coined the term by stirring a drink with a souvenir rooster tail. But James Fenimore Cooper's 1821 novel *The Spy* (set in the 1780s) has her as a military widow running a hotel at the same Westchester location.

In *The Savoy Cocktail Book* (1930), author Harry Craddock provides a possible cock (and bull) tale tracing "cocktail" to the early nineteenth century, with tensions between the southern branch of America's Army and Mexico's King Axolotl VIII. A U.S. general, attempting to forge a truce at Axolotl's Pavilion, assented to the king's offer to have a drink. A beautiful woman suddenly greeted him with a golden cup that brimmed with an aromatic potion. The king and the general were confused over who should take it; the woman, sensing a potentially embarrassing situation, bowed and drank it herself. From there the conference was smooth and successful, but upon leaving, the general insisted he know the mysterious woman's name. When Axolotl responded that it was his daughter Coctel, the grateful general pledged that his army would have her name honored and immortalized.

Going from battlefields to recreational sadism, there are reports of a "cock's ale" distributed at cockfights. The bird would be parboiled, flayed, and pulverized; lumped with three pounds of raisins, mace, and cloves; blended with ten gallons of ale in a canvas sack; then left to ferment for up to nine days. In *A New Dictionary of the Canting Crew* (1698), the following definition appears: "Cockale, pleasant drink, and said to be provocative."

H. L. Mencken, a raconteur on the subject, reported in *The American Language* that "cocktail" possibly refers to the liquor barrel drippings or "cock-tailings" mixed into a single container and turned into drinks sold at lower prices. The French also lay claim to the term, insisting that Antoine Peychaud, an eighteenth-century New Orleans apothecary of French descent, served brandy tonics in eggcups, which his native language calls *coquetiers*.

The word *cocktail* appeared for the first time in print on May 13, 1806. An editor of the Hudson, New York, publication *Balance and Columbian Repository* responded to a reader's query with a politically partisan answer:

"Cocktail is a stimulating liquor composed of spirits of any kind, sugar, water and bitters—it is vulgarly called bittered sling and is supposed to be an excellent electioneering potion, inasmuch as it renders the heart stout and bold, at the same time that it fuddles the head. It is said, also, to be of great use to a Democratic candidate: because, a person having swallowed a glass of it, is ready to swallow anything else."

In their 1863 book *Cups and Their Customs,* Henry Porter and George Roberts preferred to call cocktails "sensation-drinks." William Terrington's 1869 tome *Cooling Cups and Dainty Drinks* claims: "Cocktails are compounds very much used by 'early birds' to fortify the inner man." An 1883 entry from *Patsy McDonough's Bar-keeper's Guide* (published in Rochester, New York) connects cocktail time with the cock's crow: "The Cocktail is a very popular drink. It is most frequently called for in the morning and just before dinner; it is sometimes taken as an appetizer; it is a welcome companion on fishing excursions and travelers often go provided with it on a railroad journey."

Despite the warring claims as to its origins, the cocktail has always represented more than just a drink. It became a ritual occasion, depending not just on its mind-altering properties but on the shape of the glass in which it was served, the ceremonial antics of the bartender serving it, and the occasion for its consumption. Whoever indulged in rickeys, fizzes, juleps, cobblers, daisies, shrubs, flips, and toddies joined a regal tableau of dedicated fashion followers. Just holding a cocktail conferred monetary, intellectual, even spiritual status. Jack London, who grew up on such "poor-men's drinks" as straight whiskey, had encountered cocktails for the first time as a pecuniary symbol. When he published his first book, several Alaskan members of the San Francisco Bohemian Club treated him to witty conversation in swanky leather chairs with Highballs mixed from an array of choice bourbon.

There are, of course, sticky bits of official nomenclature that technically separate a cocktail proper from something like the "aperitif," which is usually a European-influenced, wine-based libation. Still, since these drinks are also part of cocktail time and at cocktail venues, practical simplicity merits their inclusion in any legitimate discussion *about* or *with* cocktails.

Cocktails started to get true celebrity status in the nineteenth century. Consider the Mint Julep's place in Americana. Though John Milton had alluded to something like it back in 1634 as "this cordial Julep," the libation originated in 1803, when John Davis, a traveler from Britain and a Virginia plantation tutor, defined a julep as "a dram of spiritous liquor that has mint in it, taken by Virginians of a morning." The formula evolved into the simple operation of putting several sprigs of mint into a tumbler with a spoonful of sugar and equal parts of peach and regular brandy. After filling the rest of the tumbler with crushed ice, its connoisseur could savor the concoction as the ice melted. It was so well received that the 1806 Webster's dictionary defined it as "a kind of liquid medicine," and Henry Clay later brought it across the Mason-Dixon line to Washington.

In 1888, a Henry C. Ramos came to New Orleans, bought the Imperial Cabinet Saloon, and entered the mixology archives by vigorously shaking a combination of gin, powdered sugar, orange-flower water, lemon and lime juices, egg white, cream, and seltzer water and pouring out the ethereal Ramos Gin Fizz. This ornate anecdote contrasts with the less imaginative account of Patrick Gavin Duffy, a bartender who, in 1885, purportedly mixed some whiskey with ice and soda and deemed it the Highball. It was one day destined to be the favorite cocktail of the rakish Louisiana governor Huey Long.

The original Daiquiri allegedly got its name in honor of a village near Santiago, Cuba, after the 1898 Spanish-American War. Jennings Cox was the legendary inventor, an American engineer for the Pennsylvania Steel Company and Cuba's Spanish-American Iron Company. During the sweltering summer of 1896, Cox was at a loss concerning what to serve some important visitors, having run out of gin. Reluctant to serve them straight rum, he devised a combination of lime juice and sugar to leaven it. Soon American miners visiting the island were sure to have at least one of his concoctions. Admiral Lucius Johnson of the U.S. Navy commemorated his love of Daiquiris and his acquaintanceship with Jennings Cox by bringing the drink to the United

States and to the Washington, D.C., Army and Navy Club. There, a brass plaque commemorates Cox at the club's Daiquiri Lounge.

The Flowing Bowl (an 1892 drink recipe book) described "la Creole," a drag-queen relative to the Daiquiri with this crowning touch: "Ornament with fruits in season, put a little scoop of ice cream on top, and serve." But the credit for the Daiquiri's first official printed mention goes to F. Scott Fitzgerald in his 1920 novel *This Side of Paradise*.

The most multifarious and contradictory cocktail lore surrounds the Martini's origins. Two accounts trace it to San Francisco. In one, a bartender happened onto it through serendipity at the city's Palace Hotel just before World War I. A livelier version dates further back, to the late 1800s, when the famous bartender Jerry Thomas, tending San Francisco's Occidental Bar, mixed a variation of gin and vermouth for a traveler anticipating a ferry ride along the Bay to a small town called Martinez. Martinez residents reversed the story, however, by claiming a miner was traveling from their town to San Francisco in 1870 and drank a concoction devised by local bartender Julio Richelieu.

Others credit the drink to the Italian vermouth maker Martini & Rossi. The drink was called a "Martinez" in O. H. Byron's *The Modern Bartender's Guide* (1884), which claims the drink is simply a Manhattan with gin replacing whiskey. Four years later, the term "Martini"

officially appeared in Harry Johnson's *New and Improved Illustrated Bartender's Manual or How to Mix Drinks of the Present Style*. A certain Martini di Arma di Taggia also credited himself with inventing the dry Martini at New York's Knickerbocker Club for John D. Rockefeller in 1912.

An even more historically intriguing and dubious Martini link is to a certain Sergeant Martinez of George Custer's Seventh Calvary. During the 1876 Battle of Little Bighorn, Martinez managed to avoid the skirmish with the Sioux. He was instead reassigned to Baltimore's Fort McHenry where, probably subject to more idle time, he supposedly entertained himself by inventing the Martini and flattered himself by giving it his moniker.

At the 1867 Paris Exposition, the multiheaded Whore of Babylon got reincarnated as a late-nineteenth-century American bar, replete with silver American Eagles for his/her crown and sensuous protrusions of siphon tubes dispensing liquid luster. Even England finally ceded to the New World propaganda when a British journalist admitted enjoying the dribble of "moustache twisters," "cobblers," "smashers," and "corpse revivers."

When not insinuating genitalia, the cocktail had come to symbolize the dirty little joke played on the world when the Industrial Revolution vaunted the art of combining separate components on an assembly line and calling it a product. The cocktail became a mascot for an era when mass production, pulp novels, star aesthetes, and the pioneer cinema portended modern life's frights and joys. Into the twentieth century, the cocktail was the portable melting pot, America's calico contribution to modern civilization, so tantalizing and so pure it was bound to connote all things evil and holy.

THE SOCIAL JUGGERNAUT.

Temperance Theology.
Elmer Gantry, the travel-
ing-salesman-turned-
preacher in Sinclair
Lewis's novel, got his
evangelical calling while
inebriated in a saloon. He
is one of many examples
linking alcohol's transcendental effects to some of
the delirious fire and
brimstone visions of many
Prohibitionists throughout
the nineteenth and early
twentieth centuries. The
Anti-Saloon League may
have been "born of God,"
but it resembled a down-
right devilish sideshow of
fanatic ranters. Temper-
ance theologians betrayed
an unholy alliance between
liquor and the Lord, a
bond that bolsters Lord
Byron's claim:

> There's nought, no
> doubt, so much the
> spirit calms
> As rum and true religion.

("The Social Juggernaut,"
engraving by M. Woolf:
Collection of the New-
York Historical Society)

3

Demon Rum and Angel's Tit

We could never abolish the use of liquor, until we made reality into something people didn't want to run away from, as children "play hookey" from a badly managed school.

—Upton Sinclair, *The Wet Parade*

Thornton Wilder's play *Our Town* presented the pastoral calm of a New England community in the early 1900s. Being himself a savvy writer with a keen eye for the encroaching big-city ways, he offset the callow citizens of Grover's Corners with Simon Stimson, a man who "ain't made for small town life." Stimson was the village drinker and Congregational church organist, who staggered about the village at night, had a load on his mind, and eventually hung himself in his attic. His dour countenance, tippler's lifestyle, and sinful suicide were a foreboding, a message from beyond that incomprehensible and frightening forces were closing in on this once immaculate Protestant enclave.

Many years before such modern satanic techniques as

subliminal advertising and audio backmasking, the demons looming over Grover's Corners picked Stimson, a man appointed to play the angels' music but whose demonic possession would spread to all the Grover's Corners of the nation. Monsters and incubi of many forms would materialize in the pornographic imaginations of Prohibitionists who saw fire and brimstone in those Jezebel Juleps, Crimson Cobblers, and the Demon Rum.

Prohibition had been a constant boil on America's legislative fundament since the Civil War. President Lincoln responded to a Prohibition advocate's plaint about General Grant's affinity for the bottle by asking one of his men to find out Grant's favorite whiskey brand so that he could furnish it to the rest of his generals. In 1842, Lincoln also considered drinking a sign of national maturity when "we found intoxicating liquor recognized by everybody, used by everybody, repudiated by nobody." He went on: "It is true that even then it was known and acknowledged that many were greatly injured by it; but none seemed to think the injury arose from the use of a bad thing, but from the abuse of a very good thing."

Until supplanted by whiskey, rum was the favored ogre. Long before America enjoyed such wonders as Planter's Punch and the Zombie, temperance advocates were successful in their campaign to stigmatize Demon Rum, thanks partly to its unwholesome association with the slave trade in the years when the New World used it to barter with Africa. According to Devonshire lingo, the term *rum* supposedly means "great tumult," a point that sermonizers exploited when producing many voluminous testimonials with such titles as *The Story of an Alcohol Slave, as Told by Himself* and *Confessions of a Moderate Drinker.*

The hysterical teetotalers and religious fanatics, the Woman's Christian Temperance Union, and the Anti-Saloon League were gently persuasive to God-fearing legislators. Temperance theologians, both clerical and lay, were a fruity assortment bent on neutralizing liquor with snake-oil sermons and antitippler terrorism. Though famous for his traveling circus, Phineas Taylor Barnum turned Prohibition into a real-life sideshow while serving as mayor of Bridgeport, Connecticut. In his 1875 message to the town's Common Council, Barnum proclaimed: "Spiritous liquors of the present day are so much adulterated and doubly poisoned that their use fires the brain and drives their victims to madness, violence and murder."

In their attempt to harass the very men who sought the bottle to escape wifely moralism, temperance ladies would loiter outside of saloons, wailing such slogans as "Jesus the Water of Life Will Give." Among the most notorious was Carry Nation, Prohibition's answer to Lizzie Borden. She may have resembled Whistler's mother with her white bonnet and wire-rimmed spectacles, but all semblance of matronly serenity ended when she began sabotaging the streets of her Kansas town in the early 1900s, attacking saloons with the hatchet that rarely left her side.

By the late nineteenth century, individual states were already enacting their own à la carte Prohibition laws. By the early 1900s, even esteemed authors railed against the evils of drink. Jack London, who had a fair share of alcohol binges during his youthful seafaring escapades, became a turncoat in his later years by wholeheartedly embracing teetotaler politics. His scathing book *John Barleycorn,* with its comparison of alcohol to "maggots crawling" in his brain, proved such a potent weapon that the *Saturday Evening Post* serialized it before it became a 1913 best-seller.

In *John Barleycorn,* London admits that in his youth, the cocktail possessed for him a "kindly, genial glow": "A cocktail or several, before dinner, enabled me to laugh wholeheartedly at things which had long since ceased being laughable. The cocktail was a prod, a spur, a kick, to my jaded mind and bored spirits." But the book was ultimately a forum for his discussion of what he called the "White Logic," that state of mind brought on by the white-lightning high when the mind totters on a "black abyss" of "spectral syllogisms," when all human identity is exposed as a ruse, and even mankind's most noble endeavors lose their "godly" glimmer.

The Our Towns of the New World started feeling more of an alcohol urgency around the time that a profusion of ethnic whites—particularly Irish and Italian—started pressing against the Protestant fortress. London describes his first intoxication as a lad at the hands of a "dark eyed" Italian who struck such fear in him that he could not refuse his offer of a glass of wine.

London went on to take more than one glass of wine. He chugged libations of many persuasions and had his share of swell times doing so. When he started earning good royalties from his writing, he bragged about a rather effete practice of having an Oakland bartender make cocktails in bulk and ship them to his comfortable ranch in the Valley of the Moon. Since London exploited the art of drinking as far as he could, his mea culpa in *John Barleycorn* seems the raging of a death-bed convert who jumped on the wagon too late and is all too ready to deny more moderate drinkers their cocktail rights.

Prohibition sentiments grew more strident with mounting industrialism and migrations of populations from rural areas to cities. World War I also fed into the sentiments, particularly with the proliferation of brewers with German names. Moreover, Prohibitionists had intertwined their cause with the war economy. Foods and other supplies were being rationed to support the American forces as well as the armies of England and Europe. Using vital grains to make alcohol beverages was, therefore, deemed by many a wartime heresy. There was soon talk of the government using its war powers to ban liquor manufacture.

Years later, the war against liquor started blending with sentiments against Catholicism. When "wet" Democrat Al Smith announced his candidacy for president in 1928 against "dry" Republican Herbert Hoover, Baptist Pastor J. A. Scarboro condemned the Roman Catholic Smith as a bastion for "The Devil's crowd—Catholics, political demagogues, brewers, bootleggers, prostitutes . . ." After Smith won the nomination at the Democratic Convention in Houston, an Alabama Representative named "Cotton Tom" Heflin (who held Prohibition as dear to his heart as the belief in WASP supremacy) walked out, charging that his party was being run by "the liquor interests, Tammany and the Roman Catholic machine."

Not only conservative curmudgeons joined the dry bandwagon. In truth, many feminists, Christian pacifists, moral "progressives," and others of the more "cosmopolitan" mind-set also fought the cause at one time or another. One such muckraker group, the Women's National War Economy League, pledged a list of Calvinistic self-denials, among them the vow "to abstain from cocktails, highballs and all expensive wines." Jack London, who had once celebrated saloons as a reprieve "from the narrowness of women's influence into the wide free world of men," broke from his customary macho ideals by endorsing woman's suffrage, assuming that the petticoat vote would favor Prohibition. In 1913, the Webb-Kenyon law, a preliminary test version of the Volstead Act (which would soon provide the means for enforcing Prohibition), got backing from about as many "progressive" senators as there were conservatives opposing it.

On January 17, 1920, at 12:01 A.M., the Eighteenth Amendment and the Volstead Act had formally commenced, making it a felony to sell, manufacture, deliver, transport, or traffic in any beverage containing 0.5 percent alcohol or more. The next day, the 50-50 Club opened over a New York City garage on West Fiftieth Street, sating its members with clandestine whiskey. Bartenders and patrons of New York's Park Avenue Club mourned by displaying a casket full of black bottles. There would soon be a new custom of serving patrons "setup" trays with glasses, ice, garnishes, juices, syrups, and other condiments to go with the illicit bottle that they were expected to smuggle in jackets and hip pockets.

Upton Sinclair, a socialist and social reformer who would one day run for California governor, published his novel *The Wet Parade* in 1931. Antidrink and anti-Prohibition at the same time, he explored how the Volstead Act engendered a significant rise in political corruption and organized crime. The story centers on the Chilcotes, a family of Southern gentry beset by self-destructive drinkers, a cynical writer, and a militant teetotaler. Transported to New York City, the Chilcotes encounter skid row bums forced to go cold turkey, the more privileged who buy off the authorities and flout the law with "whoopee parties" and "pleasure districts," and the impregnable racketeer armies able to bribe public officials, traffic in smuggled liquor, and secure their profits by seeing that the Volstead Act remained ironclad.

The dawn of Prohibition witnessed the miraculous obfuscation of sacred and profane. The legal censure turned cocktails into a ritual of indulgence and absolution combined. Substances once considered vile were soon gussied up in fancy glasses with ornate combinations of ingredients and titles. They got more mystifying and appealing as their legal standing grew more illicit and their manufacture and sale more tawdry. According to historian Henry Lee in his 1963 book *How Dry We Were,* "In the fall of 1928, while the Yankees were taking the first three games from the Cardinals in the World Series, some 32 poison alcohol fatalities were counted just in a few days on New York's Lower East Side."

Thanks to the legal strictures, ordinary fun lovers became creative outlaws, converting a contraband substance into something frothy and heavenly. Talking to a national magazine, Prohibition's dubious messiah Al Capone delivered a sobering line: "They call Capone a bootlegger—yes, it's bootleg while it's on the trucks, but when you're host at a club, in the locker room of your country club or on the Gold Coast where they serve it to you on a silver platter, it's hospitality."

Capone's efforts also inspired a lively vocabulary. The term *bootlegging* originated from the practice of smuggling whiskey inside boots, and the word *moonshine* denoted the stills that usually ran at night when least detectable. When there were no charred oak barrels to give whiskey its brown color, the name *white lightning* became commonplace. *Teetotaler,* on the other hand, allegedly derived from a temperance society in New York that required all neophytes in the organization to place the letter *T* beside their signed names to indicate they had consigned themselves to "total" abstinence.

One significant cultural leap was America's wholehearted embrace of gin. Not until Prohibition did gin, with its easy-to-make properties, become a true liquor contender. In the late sixteenth century, a Dutch professor of medicine named Franz de la Boë (often referred to as

Speakeasy. Many believed Prohibition came about through women's suffrage. But once drinking was forbidden, women emerged not as teetotalers but as the cocktail culture's supreme adherents. Previously barred from male drinking rituals, women became speakeasy showcases. Their refined mannerisms had even inspired cultured urban men to adopt more graceful affectations in a nightclub, a venue so much more rarefied than a saloon. ("Speakeasy," lithograph by J. W. Golinkin: Collection of the New-York Historical Society)

Franciscus Sylvius) invented the substance as a blood purifier that could be sold at apothecaries.

Gin got its name from *jenever,* the Dutch term for the juniper berries added to the beverage during redistillation. British soldiers stationed in the Lowlands were so intrigued by the nostril-burning and stomach-warming properties of what they called "Dutch Courage" that they brought it back to the Isles. Gin became a recreational indulgence in England from the time of William of Orange to the notorious nineteenth-century Victorian gin palaces.

America once denounced it as "Mother's Ruin," but gin was so simple to make in a bathtub that the upper classes who once despised it suddenly championed it. Enter the Martini!

In 1917, the *New York Sun* contributed some apocryphal anthropology when it uncovered knowledge about Dri Mart Ini, an ancient Egyptian god of thirst, a priest of the goddess Isis, depicted "shaking a drink in a covered urn of glass while the 15th pharaoh of the dynasty of Lush is shown with protruding cottony tongue quivering with pleasurable expectation."

Fancier drinks, already popular at the turn of the century, were embraced with even greater fervor—one more proof that Hollywood's fantasy world spilled over into cocktail folklore with various drinks named after favorite body parts or silent screen stars. One and a half ounces of pineapple juice mixed with one and a half ounces of Puerto Rican rum, a few dashes of grenadine, and maraschino liqueur were all it took to create a Mary Pickford. The recipe for another afterdinner drink involved two-thirds maraschino liqueur covered by an aureole of one-third cream, and topped with a maraschino cherry nipple—the combination was aptly called an Angel's Tit.

Prohibition changed the venue and the social politics by which people drank. From the time of the Revolutionary War, the tavern was as much an excuse for bonding as it was for bibbing. Around the world in general and in America in particular, drinking places were almost always fraternal. Theodore Roosevelt could boast about drinking as part of manhood's manifest destiny, even though office jobs and other less "manly" occupations were multiplying all around him.

Sweet irony. Enfranchised women, considered Volstead's lethal weapon, would soon give the twenties cocktail culture a flapper-happy, coeducational sheen. The rise of speakeasies coincided with the new custom whereby women and men staggered along the tippler's abyss together.

4

"Giggle Water"

Nobody we know does anything but drink in this crazy
town . . .

—Carl Van Vechten, *Parties*

The Roller Coaster Years, the Jazz Age, the era of
flappers, vamps, rumrunners, drunken parties, and
dance-hall gigolos. A time when emotions and
thoughts rose and plunged like the jagged stock market. In
The Wet Parade, Upton Sinclair described the years as
"thumping tom-toms and rattle of drums, wails and shrieks
that sent shivers up and down your spine, rhythms that suggested a man dancing with his knees out of joint. The genial
old German formula: 'Wein, Weib, und Gesang' had been
translated and modernized into 'Gin, janes, and jazz.'"

Alcohol's new contraband status gave drinking a ritual
allure that spawned nightclubs, café societies, speakeasies,
and an everpresent mobster ambience—all adding up to a
celebrity culture that would outlast Prohibition and the

Depression and continue throughout the twentieth century. Danger, scandal, and a relentless desire to live only for the present inspired a satirist to think up the quintessential twenties cocktail: Soak three men with three chorus girls in champagne, squeeze them into an automobile at midnight, "add a dash of joy, and a drunken chauffeur. Shake well. Serve at 70 miles an hour. Chaser: a coroner's inquest."

In 1930, author Carl Van Vechten dedicated his final novel, *Parties,* to a retrospective on these years. He saw it through the eyes of New York hedonists with pseudo-European airs traipsing from party to party. Engrossed in their Sidecars and Pernod, they grew increasingly over-sexed, pessimistic, and obsessed by tabloid murders they were too spineless to commit themselves.

John Dos Passos presented Prohibition as an ironic backdrop to a soused society in his novel *Manhattan Transfer.* Throughout, he alludes to how cocktails establish some meager context in otherwise disoriented lives. While authorities impose a halfhearted sanction against them, the cocktails are relaxing and uniting the people. One important scene occurs when a character has an "absinthe cocktail" for breakfast at Mouquin's restaurant: "The smell of absinthe sicklytingling grew up like the magician's rosebush out of Jimmy's glass. He sipped it wrinkling his nose. 'As a moralist I protest,' he said. 'Whee, it's amazing.'"

Enjoying an absinthe cocktail during Prohibition was a double taboo since absinthe was made illegal even before the Volstead Act. Ernest Hemingway, in *For Whom the Bell Tolls,* describes the hallucinogenic wormwood concoction as "that opaque, bitter, tongue-numbing, brain-warming, stomach-warming, idea-changing liquid alchemy." Dos Passos, as *Manhattan Transfer*'s narrator, witnesses quite a few otherwise docile citizens willfully break the law to alter their minds. In one instance, he concludes: "The only thing an incomplete organism can do is drink."

The literary world was awash in spirits. H. L. Mencken, who referred to himself as "ombibulous," insisted on avoiding drinks by daylight but never refusing one after dark. He also once hired a mathematician to calculate every conceivable cocktail combination, arriving at 17,864,292,788, and boasted of having sampled 273 at random and liking them all.

Among the most favored literary cocktail legends is that of the Algonquin Round Table. The Round Table assembled just in time for Prohibition, when press agent John Peter Toohey decided to exact lighthearted revenge on drama critic Alexander Woollcott. Woollcott had apparently refused to write a story promoting Toohey's client Eugene O'Neill. So in June of 1919, Toohey and cronies planned a gag luncheon with the pretense of honoring Woollcott on his return from covering World War I. They instead attempted to infuriate him by purposely misspelling his name on the invitation and subjecting him to lashing litotes and waspish witticisms. The savvy Woollcott went along with the hijinx and helped launch a regular consortium of such chic scribblers as Dorothy Parker, Edna Ferber, Heywood Broun, Robert E. Sherwood, screenwriter George S. Kaufman, illustrator Neysa McMein, and actor

Robert Benchley, who supposedly thought up the quote, "Let's get out of these wet clothes and into a dry Martini."

Since the Algonquin's owner, Frank Case, had stopped serving liquor a year before the Volstead Act had passed, any Round Table drinking would have been done (at least officially) outside. The charitable Case had taken a shine to these relatively penniless pen pushers and eventually reserved a table for them in the famed Rose Room, where they remained on display for visiting columnists and other newsmakers. According to Barbara McGurn, an Algonquin public-relations manager who started visiting the Algonquin to drink hot chocolate when she was ten: "The Round Table people had a daily routine. They would have lunch at the Round Table, then, later in the afternoon, go to see Neysa McMein, who had a still in her bathroom. Then they'd go to the theater and later visit Tony's, their favorite speakeasy. There was also Polly Adler's, a combination speakeasy and brothel that both men and women would visit."

In Greenwich Village, many bohemians had to forsake corner saloons for clandestine front operations at the nearby grocery, pharmacy, tobacco shop, or barbershop. Many of the more financially privileged slaked their thirst by heading for the Continent, primarily for Paris. Whether on the Left or Right Bank, Ezra Pound, Gertrude Stein, Ernest Hemingway, and their minions joined other monied American tourists at such exile outposts as Harry's Bar or the Ritz. Comparing it to the Village, author Frederick J. Hoffman said of the Left Bank: "True, there was the same easy and carefree atmosphere, but here drinking was in the open, at the sidewalk cafés—interesting and new drinks with a predictable alcohol content and an honest label."

If any stereotyped label fit the twenties bon vivant, it was *oral-aggressive*. Drinking helped to open portals to an underworld of forbidden desires and motives. Many of the bohemians fancied themselves the gatekeepers of the irrational, and accused middle-class denizens of having prissy hang-ups. But even in the twenties, these rebels were already yesterday's news, holdovers from the nineteenth-century aesthetes who assumed art would take care of all life's ills.

Far from flouting the Protestant work ethic, cocktail culture worked as its hedonistic complement—the holy grail dangling at the American dream's terminus. Elam Harnish in Jack London's novel *Burning Daylight* rises from Oregon yokel to urbane executive in a climb to power that intensifies with Harnish's mounting taste for Martinis. This was also a time when Joseph Patrick Kennedy took full advantage of the Jazz Age by carousing with under-world bootleggers, tinkering with the stock market, producing such scandalous Hollywood bagatelles as Erich von Stroheim's *Queen Kelly,* and siring future senators and a president.

F. Scott Fitzgerald once claimed: "I shocked a rising young businessman by suggesting a cocktail before lunch. In 1929 there was liquor in half the downtown offices, and liquor in half the large buildings." Fitzgerald, who once confessed a liking for "glittering expensive things," cast his midwestern-bred antihero Jay Gatsby in his novel *The Great Gatsby* as the lord of opulent parties and bootlegging intrigues. Gatsby nurtured his quick path to wealth not just from prolonged obsession with old flame Daisy but out of a deeper love affair with what the novel's narrator calls "the service of a vast, vulgar, and meretricious beauty."

Clara Bow may have called it "a longer word for joy," but the American cocktail is most fascinating for the Jekyll and Hyde transformation it inspired in the workaday bourgeois character. The compliant diurnal worker needed only a few sips of the forbidden giggle water to become a nocturnal hellion. Cocktail parties may have flaunted high-society pretensions, but ultimately they stayed successful by reinforcing middle-class notions of "the good life."

Prohibition's effect on cities was cataclysmic since, by the twenties, more than 50 percent of Americans were urbanites. Prior to World War I, hosts rarely served drinks before dinner. By 1929, there were at least 120 cocktail recipes with an almost equal number of prescribed domestic occasions to go with them.

Nothing better captures this savoir faire than some of the era's popular songs. In 1922, Cole Porter, who took great pleasure in switching his cocktail haunts from Hollywood to Paris, composed "Cocktail Time" for the musical *Mayfair and Montmartre*. "Two Little Babes in the Wood," another Porter song for the 1924 production *Greenwich Village Follies*, rhymed "fountain of youth" with "gin and vermouth." Irving Berlin's "I'll See You in C-U-B-A" satirized how the wealthy often crossed over into Havana to enjoy a few duty-free and jail-free refreshments.

One of the leading nightlife personalities was Texas Guinan. Guinan (born in Waco, hence her nickname) was a vaudeville performer and silent two-reeler film star who usually played a cowgirl counterpart to William S. Hart. She attained her true stardom in 1923, as hostess in New York's El Fey. With her bleached blonde hair, flawless false teeth, mounds of makeup, brash manner, and husky singing voice, she instantly earned the moniker "Queen of the Nightclubs."

When Walter Winchell was a budding Broadway columnist, Guinan took him under her wing to tutor him about the big-city demimonde. Winchell would soon call that crowd "gintellectuals" and the speakeasies they inhabited "sotto voce parlors." Winchell, a man of many neologisms and opinions, would frequent the Stork Club to witness every rising and falling star's idiosyncrasies, privy at all times to numerous cocktail scandals.

One such scandal involved Broadway producer Earl Carroll, best known for his revue entitled *Earl Carroll's Vanities*. He had previously given a wild party where a young showgirl was allegedly persuaded to bathe naked in a tub full of champagne. The incident was brought to trial in May 1926, and Carroll was convicted of perjury for giving false testimony about the incident.

These golden days of nightclub glamour harbored many tales in which the cocktail, in its multifarious forms, loomed over real-life characters as a shadowy religious icon. Such personalities as George Gershwin, Moss Hart, and Edna Ferber reportedly caroused in George S. Kaufman's private salon while Vachel Lindsay chanted exotic verse to a cocktail shaker's rhythm. Torch singer Helen Morgan would sit atop a piano at New York's Chez Morgan, a speakeasy that mobster Lucky Luciano had opened and dedicated to her.

Some of the most novel clubs emerged during the twenties. Joseph Urban designed New York's Park Avenue Club, known for its octagonal bar and envelope of mirrors running from floor to ceiling. The Merry-Go-Round at East Fifty-sixth Street had carousel horses that made a complete eleven-minute orbit around the bar all night.

The club owners themselves, many of whom came from humble backgrounds, were major figures in the new culture. John Perona, who opened El Morocco in 1931, was an Italian immigrant and former Knickerbocker Grill busboy. Sherman Billingsley was a native of Oklahoma who, with his brothers, sold bootleg liquor in a drugstore and later served time in Leavenworth for rumrunning in Detroit. By the late twenties, Billingsley was proprietor of the Stork Club, a place that achieved instant celebrity when Walter Winchell dubbed it the "New Yorkiest spot in New York."

In the twenties and very early thirties, such club owners faced a world as dangerous as the Old West. Billingsley lost much of his club's equipment during one 1931 govern-

Cole Porter and Elsa Maxwell. Songwriter Cole Porter and legendary party-matron Elsa Maxwell often held cocktail court in the era when celebrities first usurped the role of traditional statesmen. Among Porter's cocktail songs: "Make It Another Old Fashioned, Please," "Say It with Gin," "Absinthe Drip," "Cocktail Time," "Drink Drink Drink," and "Here's a Cheer for Dear Old Ciro's." (AP/Wide World Photos)

ment raid and was kidnapped for three days and held for $25,000 ransom when he did not cooperate with racketeers trying to skim his profits.

When Prohibition ended in April 1933, Walter Winchell was successful in getting New York's Board of Estimate to rescind a 4:00 A.M. curfew that was put in place to keep speakeasies in check. Casino de Paree owner Billy Rose hosted a celebration. In the Algonquin Hotel lobby, Clifton Webb and Marilyn Miller celebrated the Volstead Act's death during their starring stint in *As Thousands Cheer.* Minsky's, the famous New York burlesque house, had a sign at its entrance reading "We'll Take Gin." President Roosevelt, an ardent gin lover, most likely celebrated by pouring himself the first legal White House Martini.

With the postflapper era, the cocktail atmosphere attained a legally sanctioned majesty. Café society promoted a posh lifestyle despite the hundreds of impoverished citizens selling apples and pencils on street corners. New York's Rainbow Room had opened in 1934 to the sounds of Ray Noble. Sherman Billingsley unveiled the first contour bar, the first canopied entranceway, and the first champagne cocktail when he moved the Stork Club from West Fifty-eighth to East Fifty-third Street.

Café society became the first major fad in a new age of legal liquor. Here monied socialites mixed with "common" showfolk and publicity hounds, all vying for a place at the photo-friendly table. The media mogul, not the aristocrat, determined social concerns. Neal Gabler writes in *Winchell: Gossip, Power and the Culture of Celebrity:* "For

FDR's Cocktail Shaker Set. Once Prohibition was finally lifted, cocktails occasionally put a macabre razzle-dazzle into political affairs. A Martini devotee, President Roosevelt brought juniper juice to the international bargaining table when he joined Prime Minister Churchill and Marshal Stalin at a late 1943 conference in Tehran to discuss strategies for winning the war and dividing up the spoils. Soviet Foreign Secretary Vyacheslav Molotov (whose namesake denotes another kind of cocktail) warned that the Germans might be plotting to assassinate all three leaders. The threat, however, did nothing to cramp Roosevelt's style as he reportedly fixed Stalin what is perhaps the first "dirty" Martini, consisting of two parts gin, one part vermouth, and a dose of olive brine. Though Stalin, accustomed to Russian vodka, claimed the Martini was cold to his stomach, the occurrence prompted a Roosevelt official to describe those years as the "four martinis and let's have an agreement" era. (Photograph courtesy of Franklin D. Roosevelt Library, Hyde Park, N.Y.)

most Americans, 'cafe society' immediately triggered images of women in smart gowns and men in satin-collared tuxedoes, of tiered nightclubs undulating in the music of swell bands, of cocktails and cigarettes, of cool talk and enervated elegance, all of which made cafe society one of those repositories of dreams at a time when reality seemed treacherous."

The famed Brown Derby in Hollywood was reportedly designed with banquettes made of brown leather, laid out in semicircles so that all of the patrons could gawk at one another no matter which table they took. In Budd Schulberg's novel *What Makes Sammy Run?,* one of its characters rhapsodizes "that one of the things which distinguished the old Brown Derby on Wilshire was the way guests at one end of the room could hear distinctly every word being said at the other, because of the trick acoustics of the dome-shaped ceiling. And that it always seemed as if all Hollywood must be covered by one of those Derby ceilings too."

In 1936, Meyer Quain and his sister Rachel Pinto opened New York City's famous Monkey Bar at 60 East Fifty-fourth Street. Situated beneath the ultracivilized Hotel Elysee, Meyer's establishment thrived on a contrasting, decidedly simian atmosphere. Among Eugene Zakin's ape etchings and the bar's olive-shaped stools, a white-jacketed pianist resembled an epicene veterinarian. The equally exotic El Morocco boasted an assortment of zebra-striped banquettes.

Joseph Sobol, a Broadway columnist, described these period clubs: "Dark and guarded doors opening into a spreading world of enchantment . . . a world of soft lights, seductive scents, silken music." Cranky H. L. Mencken, on the other hand, was less impressed. In 1934, he would write in the *Baltimore Sun:* "The same side-show murals on the walls, and the same cacochromatic play of lights. The same sad youths laboring the same jazz. The same middle-aged couples bumping and grunting over the dance floor like dying hogs in a miasmatic pen. The same interludes of dismal professional entertainment, with the same decayed vaudevillians. The same crooners, male and female, bawling maudlin jingles into the same mikes."

The roster of cocktail celebrities multiplied. Elsa Maxwell, columnist and New York café society doyenne, had her own room at the Waldorf gratis, and would often join Cole Porter in staging some of the most elaborate celebrity parties. She once gave a ball for an up-and-coming parvenu and adorned every female guest with a cocktail whose color matched her gown. She is also credited with the maxim, "Cocktails are society's most enduring invention."

Stories about the Hollywood cocktail circuit also abounded. Marion Davies, the famous silent screen actress and paramour to William Randolph Hearst, reportedly flaunted her wealth by sipping from a phalanx of cocktail shakers placed around her swimming pool. Errol Flynn and David Niven (infamous for barroom altercations and exploits with a variety of intoxicating substances) would eventually chip in on a Hollywood retreat nicknamed "Cirrhosis-by-the-Sea."

John Barrymore was another tippling roué whose

bottle-fed excesses showed progressively in his later films. His grandiloquent gestures, rolling eyes, and macabre hand gyrations got so pronounced that some film historians claim they can guess when he was drinking on the movie set by the number of times he blinks between lines.

Budd Schulberg's novel *What Makes Sammy Run?* addresses liquor's histrionic role on both sides of the screen. His main character, Sammy Glick, a studio mogul who finagles and cheats his way to power, embodies Hollywood's predatory movie machine. The drink becomes an inanimate liaison between people who have no other way of getting to know one another. Schulberg's narrator takes note of this connection by describing Glick's Tinseltown nightlife: "I don't think he ever drank because he liked the taste of whiskey. . . . He just went through the motions of relaxing because he was quick to discover and imitate how gentlemen of his rank were supposed to spend their leisure."

With the stage and screen as reinforcement, the thirties cocktail cult found its true "golden calf" in the silver shaker. Though a Chicago man had patented the first silver cocktail shaker in 1877, the thirties had elevated it into a deco obsession. Differing cocktail shaker styles parallel significant economic and social changes between the great wars. The otherwise reckless twenties stayed prim in its preference for old-fashioned cocktail cutlery that resembled handcrafted European tea sets. But by the late twenties and into the thirties, the Depression increased a demand for cheaper materials. They were also lightweight enough to enable sculptors to fashion them into aerodynamic curves, which made streamlining an authentic design style. With the merger of art and industry sanctioned at Chicago's 1933 Century of Progress Exposition, the cocktail shaker was no longer a rare luxury item for the few but an inexpensive household necessity.

The silver shaker offered a miniaturized reminder of the machine age's bold new Faustian lures, alchemy's base metal unleashing golden moments full of graven images and frozen poses. A 1932 advertisement for the "Napier Recipe Cocktail Shaker" depicts the shaker as a sacred megalith surrounded by adoring sycophants in posh eveningwear. Sounding less like an ad than a pagan invocation, it promises: "Henceforth—this is not facetious / Your drinks will please a Dionysos."

At the 1939 World's Fair in Flushing, New York, the supertechnologized "world of tomorrow" stood before thousands of patrons. It was a runway full of newfangled washing machines, kitchen appliances, robots instructing visitors about future kitchenware, aerodynamic sculptures, and weapons galore. But anyone looking for a high-tech escape from the streamlined excess had only to take refuge in the Hurricane Bar, where a new cocktail was introduced to the world: the Zombie.

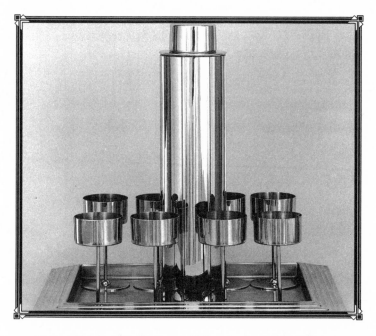

Norman Bel Geddes's Skyscraper Shaker. By the thirties, industrial designers such as Norman Bel Geddes helped bring the cult of cocktails into an era of streamlined architecture. After making this cocktail service for the Martini of Tomorrow, Bel Geddes went on to design the "Futurama" exhibit at New York's 1939 World's Fair. Another example of how gracefully drinking entered the machine age was a 1943 Seagram's V.O. Canadian ad juxtaposing the image of its whiskey with a "floating palace of dreamlike luxury" called the S.S. Futura. The caption read: "Men Who Plan beyond Tomorrow Prefer the World's Lightest Highball!" Today, Bel Geddes's original model for an aerodynamic oceanliner hangs over the Promenade Bar at New York City's Rainbow Room. (Norman Bel Geddes for Revere Co. *Cocktail Service*, Yale University Art Gallery, Stephen Carlton Clark, B.A. 1903, Fund)

5

Voices in Vermouth
(The Cocktail Crooner)

I got a request to do a song, that's dedicated to all the saloon keepers who have blown their liquor license, called "I Didn't Know What Time It Was."

—Frank Sinatra, *Pal Joey*

Choice cocktail music, like choice liquor, is best when clarified and distilled. After filtering out the excessive passion, ethnic posturing, and other raw grains, we are left with a sonic tonic that is immaculate yet potent enough to soothe the friskiest of moods. Just as the cocktail is designed to retain a modicum of order in a chaotic world, cocktail music's blend of pianos, vibraphones, guitars, and sultry ballroom orchestras is fashioned precisely to allay the nightclub's potential bedlam of bristling egos, inebriated banter, and clinking crystal. Cocktail singers emerge amid this decor as living spirits whose voices pour like silky vermouth to signal that precious moment when the dimmers grow dimmer, the spotlight glows, and the casino chatter subsides.

Crooners were the male version of this magical presence, adorning Prohibition-era starlight rooms, supper clubs, and camouflaged gambling nooks. Crooning—a method of using the voice to slide up and down the scale—has proven among the most enduring of cocktail styles. While it had influenced such popular vocalists as Rudy Vallee, "Whispering" Jack Smith, Cliff Edwards (Jiminy Cricket's voice in Walt Disney's *Pinocchio*), actor Dick Powell, Tony Bennett, Dean Martin, Vic Damone, Al Martino, Matt Monro and, of course, Sinatra, the ingenious technique had ambiguous origins. Some trace crooning to Italian bel canto, Protestant hymn, Jewish cantoring, jazz phrasing, and, most intriguing of all, the advent of microphones, allowing performers to sing in near whispers and still be heard.

However, the crooner's obvious inspiration, bubbling right below his nose, has always been the drink. The cocktail—both its aesthetics and its unique chemical interaction with human blood sugar—sets the woozy, undulating, and slow-motion sound. Tight but not drunk, slow but not listless, crooners walk a tippler's tightrope. Theirs is a feat of human grace, a performance suggesting that cocktail life can redeem us before we stagger too far.

A prime example of this style is the song "Learn to Croon," cowritten by Sam Coslow (who started out as a crooner). Bing Crosby sang it in 1931 for his first starring picture, *College Humor*. The song was the first to feature those tipsy "boo boo boo boos" that would become a trademark for Crosby and many of his crooner contemporaries. Coslow also co-composed the all-time great post-Prohibition drinking song, "Cocktails for Two." Other crooners command the distinction of helping to write some of popular music's most significant drinking ditties. Rudy Vallee contributed words to "The Stein Song," while onetime crooner Harold Arlen joined forces with Johnny Mercer to create "One for My Baby," the great cry-into-your-cocktail lament that Sinatra would immortalize.

The crooner and his cocktail ambience owe much to Los Angeles's now legendary Cocoanut Grove. Before the days of the Flamingo, the Grove placed its patrons into a distended pre-Vegas and pre-Disneyland time zone. It offered a menagerie of transplanted palm trees, exotic dancers, and Hollywood socialites—all with the elegant sounds of Gus Arnheim and His Orchestra keeping the animals subdued. By the early thirties, Arnheim's mixture of jazz and romantic string-sweep backed such budding singers as Bing Crosby. With his gliding phrases and impish charm, Crosby, to quote vocalist Kenny Allen, "didn't look like he gave a damn, and yet he still managed to make you think he did."

During Prohibition's final days in the early thirties, club patrons had to sit beside their elegant table lamps sipping (what at least seemed) denatured drinks. But the Grove's intoxicating decor more likely got people tipsy by osmosis. By many accounts, however, Crosby's pickled performances were not from contact highs. His vocal evolution reportedly coincided with his increased penchant for drinking. From time to time, when he failed to show up for important engagements, Crosby's producers reportedly had to retrieve him from speakeasies. When Cremo Cigars, a leading sponsor, took charge of Crosby's radio show, the American Tobacco Company drew up a contract requiring that the bottled muse remain off-limits.

In their book *Bing Crosby: The Hollow Man,* authors Donald Shepherd and Robert E. Slatzer relate neurosurgeon Dr. J. DeWitt Fox's eyewitness account of a Crosby supper-club performance at the Beverly Wilshire Hotel. About to sing, Crosby spewed forth neither singing nor champagne.

Enchantment, not nausea, however, fed the crooner mystique. Often draped in ceremonial white coat and tails, hovering over a round metallic microphone that resembled an antenna getting signals from the stratosphere, the crooner was akin to a technocratic sorcerer. With such songs as "Crosby, Columbo and Vallee" making them even more topical, crooners became cult figures. Professional warfare was imminent in October 1931, when the *Hollywood Reporter* suggested that Russ Columbo might surpass Crosby as the top crooner contender.

Alternately hailed as the Romeo of Songs and the Valentino of Vocalists, Columbo came onto the scene when the brilliantined Latin matinee idol rattled the cramped cage of American male identity. Whereas Crosby projected a glib, sexless, and compulsively neutral exterior, the handsome Columbo had a vulnerably sexual languor that fit well with his vermouth vibrato.

Columbo's style was uniquely hypnotic. His vocal

solos luxuriated in each distended vowel and rolled through oceanic, slow-motion tones on songs of giddy romance, erotic madness, and love-slaves. His style approximated that state of mild intoxication experienced when cocktail time just starts to take hold: The blood sugar begins to sink, the head feels light, the inhibitions subside, and the world looks so much more desirable than in the rude, sober daylight.

Like Crosby, Columbo had played the Cocoanut Grove under Arnheim. He also recorded his version of "Where the Blue of the Night Meets the Gold of the Day" just a few days before Crosby did the same and made it his theme song. Growing up a violinist with aspirations for opera, Columbo had his own band by 1931 and also played at New York's Central Park Hotel, where he showcased some of his own compositions.

One of Columbo's co-collaborations, "Prisoner of Love," became a crooner standard that Perry Como later made into a fifties hit. When Columbo sang it, he made a tearfully tipsy appeal to sweet surrender, inspiring visions of purple boudoirs, candlelight, and velvet sheets. For more adroit listeners, the song hints of gilded shackles looming overhead. While crooning some of his other compositions, Columbo gave the impression he had fallen under the same rapture and lunar delusions that captivated his audiences. "Let's Pretend There's a Moon" conjures up "the spell of moonlight bliss" that turns into literal lunacy in his signature tune, "You Call It Madness (I Call It Love)."

Columbo and fellow crooners were the elegant

Russ Columbo. Look into Russ Columbo's eyes and imagine the spell he cast on hundreds of men and women intoxicated by the heavenly combination of his voice and Prohibition liquor. Columbo was among the many crooners who challenged the traditional image of the robust singer. Crooners in general, with their suave, manicured and, at times, sexually ambiguous demeanor, emphasized a seemingly effortless singing mode. The style sometimes bordered on whispering but was ideal for environments that centered around ritual drinking. (The Music Division, The New York Public Library for the Performing Arts, Astor, Lenox and Tilden Foundations)

façade, the soft-spoken, tuxedoed swains shielding the world of casinos, the mobsters and backroom deals that continued even after Prohibition died. Art imitated life in the 1933 movie *Broadway Through a Keyhole,* in which Columbo plays a singer in love with a gangster's girl. Lowell Sherman (himself one of Hollywood's most amusing and notorious drinkers) directed the film and wasted no time stacking the cast with many of his favored cronies, including nightclub hostess Texas Guinan. The movie originated from a story suggested by Walter Winchell, a supposed real-life account of the love triangle between dancer Ruby Keeler, cantor Al Jolson, and racketeer Frank "Irish" Costello.

Russ Columbo's velvet vocalist allure was cut short by tragedy. In September 1934, just as he was becoming a leading movie star, he visited his friend Lansing Brown, a Hollywood portrait photographer, who happened to be playing with a souvenir dueling pistol he kept at his desk. While the two men conversed, Brown accidentally dropped a match into the gun and ignited a charged bullet that ricocheted off a piece of furniture and into Columbo's left eye.

At Columbo's funeral, Crosby and Lowell Sherman were among the pallbearers. Crosby would go on to romp around the world on various *Road* picture soundstages with Bob Hope and don Santa Claus outfits in holiday musicals. But Columbo rose from the ashes with posthumous glory. Dying in his prime, he left a flurry of speculations about the even greater saint he would have become if allotted more miracle time.

Columbo may have kept the balance between being soused and straight, but by the time Dean Martin recorded his slurry fifties versions of "You Belong to Me" and "Memories Are Made of This," the scales took a precarious dip. Even after the ring-a-ding-ding of forties and early fifties swing enticed velvet-coated vocalists to switch from being pompadoured princes to high-rolling heels, crooners continued to project an almost boyish nobility. It is a role that got perfected on film decades later with Al Martino's portrayal of the troubled singer Johnny Fontaine in Francis Ford Coppola's *The Godfather,* a potential hellraiser when he left the mike but a winsome poet on stage.

6

Blondes in Bottles
(Silver Shakers on the Silver Screen)

> No longer slinking,
> Respectably drinking,
> Like civilized ladies and men.
> —"Cocktails for Two,"
> from *Murder at the Vanities*

Greta Garbo spoke into the movie camera for the first time in 1930 with a cocktail call to arms: "Gimme a viskey, ginger ale on the side. And don't be stingy, baby." The film was *Anna Christie,* an adaptation of Eugene O'Neill's drama about an ex-prostitute from Sweden who comes to America to unite with her long-lost father. Throughout the story, drink is a symbol of licentiousness and character downfall. Garbo begins as a whiskey lover but after atoning for her transgressions before both her dad and husband-to-be, she becomes a rehabilitated milk drinker. Yet despite such halfhearted moralizing, the two self-satisfied male leads close the film with a toast.

By the thirties, life imitated the cinema more than

ever. This was especially true for post-Prohibition politics: Drinking became the welcomed prodigal son of vice and sex became the new focus of evil. Within a year of the Volstead Act's repeal, Hollywood imposed upon itself an even grander proscription to take its place. It came in the form of the Production Code Administration, a censorship and review board manned by a prudish Irish-Catholic named Joseph Breen.

Censorship lurked in the movie industry since the days of silents, when Hollywood began facing the scrutiny of Will Hays and his Hays Office. Such factions as the Legion of Decency and the Episcopal Committee on Motion Pictures placed increased strictures on all forms of "wayward" behavior and "questionable" ideas. By 1934, the movie industry doubled its efforts to "clean up" the cinema before the government got involved. This made Breen the Hays Office potentate.

Sex (and to a lesser extent violence) was increasingly difficult to portray on the screen without Breen's censure. The newly redeemed alcohol proved a less forbidden pleasure. A ritual cocktail scene was often the rule rather than the exception for many dramas and comedies. The cocktail evolved from a universal symbol of licentiousness into one of class and civility. It served as a combination stage prop and narrative crutch to guide both actors and viewers during some of modern America's most trying years.

Before 1934, the talkies were already redolent with cocktail cameos that often upstaged the moral lectures. In

1931, which was a pivotal year, the great D. W. Griffith made his directoral swan song with *The Struggle.* This film was a grim depiction of alcohol's corrosive effect on traditional values, with a protagonist who begins in the best of Edwardian times and descends into the Jazz Age as a skid row vagrant.

That same year, Barbara Stanwyck played a free-love advocate in *Illicit,* rejecting marriage for a scandalous affair. When at last she concedes to her priggish boyfriend's connubial wishes, she receives a bad omen when friend Joan Blondell gives her a cocktail shaker as a bridal gift. From there, her disenchantment and her husband's infidelities deliver Stanwyck into the villainous arms of former infatuate Ricardo Cortez.

Ritual drinking was also portrayed as a sign of urban panache. When Edward G. Robinson's crass hoodlum Rico in *Little Caesar* schemes and kills his way to the upper mobster echelon, he makes a point of flaunting his social status by asking his guests, "Will you have a cocktail or a dash of brandy?"

Like Hollywood, the post-Prohibition liquor industry also took to self-censorship under duress. Various distiller industry manufacturers, faced with fears that the 1933 repeal would be rescinded, forged a mutual "code of good practice" agreement not to sell liquor on radio. (This attempt to quell a lingering antiliquor mind-set later extended to television and still applies today.) By a strange coincidence, the movies became a white knight at the eleventh hour by supplying indirect advertising that promoted the cocktail's glamour, mystery, and downright refreshing properties.

One prime example is Mitchell Leisen's 1934 *Murder at the Vanities* (a filmed version of *Earl Carroll's Vanities*), which is essentially a musical murder mystery. Danish actor Carl Brisson plays the male lead and prime double-murder suspect, dogged by Victor McLaglen as the bullish detective. While the backstage treachery and finger-pointing intensifies, Brisson manages to summon up enough courage and dignity to perform the Arthur Johnston–Sam Coslow song "Cocktails for Two." It is a stage extravaganza, with Brisson sporting a top hat and tails while singing to a phalanx of smartly attired women, each of whom is accompanied by two drinks at her private candlelit table and awaiting a turn to dance.

The "Cocktails for Two" number was one of many occasions when the cocktail and its atmosphere are required to remedy otherwise grim circumstances. Director Leisen would also glamorize the drinking occasion in *The Big Broadcast of 1938* when Bob Hope, for the very first time, sings his theme song "Thanks for the Memory" to co-star Shirley Ross, over cocktails.

The Thin Man series went further by making the cocktail part of the hero's armature. Author Dashiell Hammett created the tippling ex-detective Nick Charles and his equally bibulous wife, Nora, partly to satirize his own relationship with playwright Lillian Hellman and their many hearty drinking and bickering binges. When MGM optioned to make the film in 1934, the studio made several alterations to please Breen's office. Nick (William Powell) and Nora (Myrna Loy) slept in separate beds and any overt references to sex were deleted, but the drinking remained. Nick and Nora still had their Martinis before breakfast and continued to fuel on them throughout the day to sharpen their sleuthing skills. The first time he shows up in *The Thin Man,* Nick Charles appears from behind, shaking his elixir with a memorable prescription: "A Manhattan should be shaken to a fox trot, the Bronx to a two-step, but a dry Martini must always be shaken to a waltz."

Traveling Saleslady (1935) has Joan Blondell going into business with a former bootlegger to market a toothpaste that comes in such flavors as Old-Fashioned, Martini, Manhattan, and Gin Fizz. Intent on twitting her father, himself a toothpaste magnate who insists that women and business do not mix, Blondell assumes an alias and markets the product to a rival company. She then journeys from coast-to-coast to sell "Cocktail Toothpaste" while launching a publicity blitz that causes her father's business to plummet. In the process, she falls in love with dad's publicist who (unaware he is dating the boss's daughter) sets out to steal from her the formula that has America brushing "twenty times a day."

The Breen brigade did show resistance to the liberated libation from time to time. Breen objected to Tay Garnett's 1938 screwball musical *Joy of Living* because he thought it glorified alcohol. When the film's producer ignored Breen's dictum, the *Hollywood Reporter* raised its own eyebrows by deeming the movie a "beer-drinking orgy." By 1941, realizing it could not regulate the presence of cocktails as effectively as it could sex and murder, the Production Code Administration compromised by demanding "at least one picture in which no drinking is shown for each film in which there is drinking."

Sophisticated morality tales still dwelled on drinking's "evils," but even Alfred Hitchcock's patronizing portrayal of small-town American family life in *Shadow of a Doubt* makes the cocktail seem a palatable alternative to saccharine. Thornton Wilder wrote the screenplay for this 1941 variation on *Our Town* in jeopardy. Joseph Cotten plays Uncle Charlie, the "Merry Widow" murderer who settles into quaint Santa Rosa, California, with his sister's family. When his favorite niece (Teresa Wright) catches on to his crimes, Charlie turns the screw even further by bringing a big bottle of sparkling burgundy to the family dinner. Disgusted by what she knows, the niece runs from the table and into the night with Charlie following. A forbidding neon Cocktails sign creeps into view as Charlie takes her into a nearby bar, orders a double brandy, and proceeds to browbeat this "ordinary little girl living in an ordinary little town" with one of the most nihilistic monologues in movie history.

Cocktails attained an expressionistic and depraved charm in a spate of forties and fifties movies that a coterie of French eggheads would call "film noir." Breen's Production Code forbade movies to depict exactly how a criminal cracks a safe or bombs a building, but it was not prepared to outline any sanctions against delving into psychological motives easily embedded in the settings of foggy nightclubs and the language of fated toasts. In film noir, the cocktail became the complex prism through which to glimpse the human mind's fleeting vagaries. Translucent cocktail glasses contrasted nicely with the dingy interiors, deep shadows, bleak lighting, and seductive but fatal blondes luring wiseacres to their doom. The most seasoned moviegoer needs a drink just to decipher this oblique and grim world.

In *Casablanca* (1942), the champagne cocktail symbolizes heartbreak and thwarted ambitions. Humphrey Bogart's character, Rick, encases himself in his exotic Moroccan nightclub, with World War II and Germany's imminent occupation of France as the backdrop. Rick is one of many American loners who stakes his territory yet gets confused when confronting flaky strangers and lost love Ingrid Bergman haunting him. When he first appears, Rick betrays a spiritual vacuum as empty as the champagne glass that sits beside his solitary chess game. Bogart's two most memorable lines occur in proximity to a bottle. First he flashes back to his halcyon days in Paris with Bergman as he gives his memorable "Here's looking at you, kid" toast. Once they separate, he stops drinking. But when Bergman walks into his "gin joint" and reenters his life, he breaks his dry spell and crouches next to his whiskey, browbeating Sam to play "As Time Goes By". . . "Again!"

The government's 1942 ban reserving alcohol production for smokeless gunpowder and other military supplies exhorted many Americans (growing weary of victory

Casablanca. In the alien and sometimes hostile environs of North Africa, Humphrey Bogart's disoriented character Rick encloses himself in a nightclub or, more accurately, a psychological tomb where laments of lost love and faraway homes are preserved in alcohol. Though his narcissistic, colonial instincts prompted him to name this place Rick's Café Américain, he gallantly sacrifices his love for Ingrid Bergman to interloper Paul Henreid. In this one of few restful scenes, *Casablanca*'s principal players toast to their "beautiful friendship" as the beat of Nazi stormtroopers thunders in the distance. (© 1943 Turner Entertainment Co. All Rights Reserved.)

gardens and rations) to put bootleggers in business once again. When the ban was lifted a year later, liquor sales climbed 30 percent. Hollywood's dream factories, likewise, kept on pouring with such wartime melodramas as *To Have and Have Not* (1944). Director Howard Hawks cast Bogart and Bacall together for the first time in what is in many respects a variation on the *Casablanca* theme. It is an adaptation of Ernest Hemingway's novel about Vichy French rule in the Caribbean, with Bogart as an American skipper who gets involved with a Martinique Free Speech movement and even more with Bacall. As they start liking each other, they barter for each other's favors by going back and forth between their separate hotel rooms to exchange the same unopened and infinitely suggestive wine bottle.

In postwar noir, cocktail time took on a science-fiction fatalism that made drinks more integral to the plot. In John Farrow's *The Big Clock* (1948), Ray Milland plays a crime magazine reporter who gets framed for a homicide his boss committed. The prime evidence clearing him turns out to be a cocktail napkin with a green crème de menthe stain that proves he was at a bar getting grogged on Stingers when the crime occurred. Raymond Chandler's novel *The Long Goodbye* (though not made into a film until the seventies) includes the Gimlet's fluorescent combination of gin and sweetened lime juice as a beacon for disaster. It is also the story's cocktail of choice whenever Philip Marlowe gets together with his best friend, Terry Lennox, who soon leads the detective into a maze of murders, mistaken identities, and sexual confusion.

Drinking is the preamble to practically every encounter when Bogart plays Marlowe in the 1946 film of Chandler's *The Big Sleep*. Corks start to pop in the first scene when Marlowe meets with his prospective client, General Sternwood. Sternwood's butler asks him how he likes his brandy, and Bogart retorts, "In a glass!" Director Howard Hawks took out much of the novel's grit and replaced it with cloudy Production Code coyness. Halfway into the film, Lauren Bacall (playing the elusive Mrs. Rutledge) takes Bogart's Marlowe into a nightclub housing the customary compulsive pianist, trails of cigarette smoke, and glittering glasses. Luring Marlowe further into the story's web of pornography, deceit, blackmail, and death, the enigmatic Bacall orders a Scotch Mist while Marlowe (always looking for the unadorned truth) orders "a scotch and plain water."

The cocktail courtship between Bogart and Bacall continued a year later as icing on the narrative cake in Delmer Daves's tawdry and depressing film of David Goodis's novel *Dark Passage*. Here Bogart is another framed convict accused of murder and on the lam. After surgically changing his face, battling various shady characters, and enlisting Bacall's help, he finally escapes the conspiracy by leaving the country. Only at the end does the cocktail show up as the literal dessert of paradise. In a café on the Peruvian coast (similar to Rick's Café Américain in *Casablanca*), a waiter ceremoniously walks an iced liqueur to Bogart's table. Bogart sips it, then braces as the house orchestra switches from a rhumba to a lush rendition of "You're Just

Too Marvelous"—the signal for Bacall to reappear out of the blue to join him in a dance and a happy ending.

The outcome is not so sweet for Edmund O'Brien, who plays the misbegotten shipping clerk Frank Bigelow in Rudolph Maté's *D.O.A.* (1950). Bigelow gets looped into a sinister nuclear plot while taking a rest cure in San Francisco. Bewitched by a cocktail party in the suite adjoining his at the St. Francis Hotel, he follows the revelers to a manic jive nightclub and gets drawn to an archetypal femme fatale blonde ogling him from the other end of the bar. Moving next to her, Bigelow gets distracted from the stranger spiking his bourbon and water with a luminous toxin that will soon attack his vital organs and leave him with less than one week to live.

Many characters like Bigelow would show up in similar melodramas until the midsixties, when the Production Code Administration at last folded. But *D.O.A.* portends a new kind of urban male protagonist, Mike Hammer—the champion and bane of author Mickey Spillane—who, beneath the cocksure façade, is alone in a changing postwar landscape of atomic cabals and saloon subversives.

7

Lounge

I'm heading north. El Paso, maybe. Yeah, I like El Paso:
Air-conditioned cocktail lounges, fifteen-to-one Martinis,
and mirrors that don't scare you when they look at you!
— Ava Gardner, *The Night of the Iguana*

Cocktail lounges did not impress the towering gorilla in the 1949 film *Mighty Joe Young*. Who could
blame him? American captors had whisked him
from the Africa wild to display him in an exotic New York
City nightclub called Max O'Hara's Golden Safari. His native flora and fauna were transformed into set decor. Once
proud lions now paced nervously in glass enclosures behind
a "jungle bar" that served a house drink called "King of
Beasts." While hundreds of rude patrons scrambled to snap
his photo, the hirsute hostage could stand the arrogance no
longer and smashed the place in a whirlwind tantrum befit-
ting a biblical epic.

It may have been anathema to captive animals, but
Max O'Hara's Golden Safari seemed an ideal spot for regu-

lar folk to have a Zombie or two and celebrate civilization's triumph over nature. Fortunately, there were many other safari clubs and cocktail lounges that survived in all their pagan purity.

LOUNGES? PAGANS?

The cocktail lounge offers a combination fun house and minefield. When people are drinking, the architecture and inanimate objects surrounding them merit a separate character study. Sometimes the humans can even get upstaged when the contours of the glass they are holding, the bar's geometry, the furniture and fixtures, the wall angles, carpeting, lighting, colors, piano placement, and background music all assume lives of their own.

The proper lounge can make time seem suspended and the clockwork demands beyond its walls the true illusion. Lounge legerdemain can also trigger subconscious memories of ancient pagan rites which give patrons momentary hope that they are greater than human.

VEGAS TIME

Even a mercenary gangster's mind can inspire paradise. Bugsy Siegel's plan for Las Vegas's first casino, the Flamingo, came to him during a visit to a Florida race track, when a flock of the birds soared into the sky to bring, at least according to local legend, good luck. Opening in 1945, the Flamingo headlined with such entertainers as George Raft, Xavier Cugat, and Jimmy Durante, but the initial venture failed financially. Nonetheless, Siegel had planted the seeds to what would soon become the leisure industry's mega-empire.

Robert Venturi, in a study he co-wrote called *Learning from Las Vegas,* calls Vegas gambling rooms "antiarchitectural" since they depend less on actual structure and more on camouflage. His description of a typical Vegas casino applies also to the ideal cocktail lounge: "The combination of darkness and enclosure of the gambling room and its subspaces makes for privacy, protection, concentration, and control. The intricate maze under the low ceiling never connects with outside light or outside space. This disorients the occupant in space and time. One loses track of where one is and when it is. Time is limitless, because the light of noon and midnight are exactly the same. Space is limitless, because the artificial light obscures rather than defines its boundaries." Decades before Timothy Leary preached the dynamics of set and setting for LSD sessions, lounge architects and interior designers had already manufactured the optimum altered-state environment. Along with automobile showrooms and Disneyland, *lounge* became a fifties attitude, a reinvention of anthropology that established man-made shelters as the new human wilderness.

THE TIKI TOMBS

For years, lounge designers have tried to indulge the ultracivilized by mentally transporting them to wild and exotic soundstages. In the thirties, Victor "Trader Vic" Bergeron opened a place called Hinky Dink's, which had antlers, snow-

The Cocoanut Grove, circa 1950s. This postwar Isle of Golden Dreams provides Mai Tais and palm trees to satisfy ex-servicemen nostalgic about their Pacific tours of duty. What is the reward for taming the jungle? Not an exotic dancer in a grass skirt but a white-bread dream date whose cloudy deb dress offers visions of escape into outer space. (Michael Ochs Archives, Venice, Calif.)

shoes, and other outdoorsy relics hanging from the walls. He later discovered Don the Beachcomber, a Hawaiian-style restaurant full of fishnets, floats, and anything connoting tropical island decor. He transformed his Hinky Dink's Yukon theme into a Polynesian pleasure dome with masks, seashells, and an ersatz Easter Island monolith at the entrance. Believing that "real" Polynesian food was inedible, he pampered customers with versions of what Americans would want the real thing to be like, and served up drinks with such names as the White Witch, the Suffering Bastard, and Dr. Funk of Tahiti.

Discovering exotic lands was just one of leisure technology's joys. Once soldiers came home from World War II, they delighted in surrounding themselves with the "Oriental" and Afro-Caribbean menageries in which they fought. Consider the scene in William Wyler's 1946 film *The Best Years of Our Lives* when Fredric March, playing a returning GI, complains about his travails "in jungles and around savages" yet takes his family for a night on the town to the "Pelican Club" and the "Midnite Gardens" to bask amid tropical decor, primitive beats, and spastic be-boppers.

Aural Carpeting

"The lights are low . . . the candles flicker, drawing highlights from the glasses raised hand to hand. There is warmth in the room, a feeling of closeness, of belonging . . . the special feeling of two people at a special time, in a special place . . . and, with

special music!" These opening thoughts to the liner notes of an early sixties piano compilation LP entitled *Cocktails for Two* sum up the true meaning of what is often loosely called "cocktail music."

Cocktail music—both its definition and ingredients—is as elusive as the cocktail itself. Like the drink, the music is a mixture of varying elements. It is also a functional part of modern life. If movies and dentist offices can have their background music, then certainly those seeking a bibulous breather have the right to some kind of soundtrack fit for lounges, ballrooms, and cocktail parties.

The *Oxford English Dictionary* defines a "cocktail pianist" as "a player of light, inconsequential (usu. jazz-based) background music." Much like a cocktail platter, with its diminutive wieners, crackers, and onions, the cocktail pianist's program consists of small, consumable, and not too demanding snippets comprising many musical categories and time periods. A single cocktail pianist in a single set can combine the best of classical, jazz, country, or pop.

Like the pit-pit-patter of imitation rain, cocktail music's Bacardi bossa novas and sloe gin sonatas should *complement* the staccato of cash registers, clinking glasses, sputtering bar faucets, whirring blenders, and the cocktail shaker's transcendent cadences—all supported by an air-conditioner backwash. Almost any style is appropriate as long as it is atmospheric and conforms to the rarefied standards of easy listening. It could be a Lenny Dee lounge organ, a Roger Williams piano, an Arthur Lyman calypso combo, a swooning Red Norvo xylophone, a variation on Lawrence Welk's champagne music, a Guy Lombardo ballroom orchestra, or a lounge singer.

Such ensembles as the Irving Fields Trio had sailed from romantic standard to fox-trot to satiny swing during their many appearances in the Mermaid Room at New York City's Park Sheraton. Don the Beachcomber's restaurant and bar in Waikiki was among the most successful attempts to make the music match the look. Pianist Martin Denny started featuring his exotica combo there in 1954 and later played the Shell Bar at Henry Kaiser's Hawaiian Village. There Denny's percussionist Augie Colon imitated ornate birdcalls amid vibes, gongs, drums, conch shells, and the ambience of inebriates.

It is no mere coincidence that silent movies and cocktail lounges are dominated by the piano and organ, two instruments that can approximate the melodic complexities of a song with a minimum of bulk and expense. Martin Denny's cocktail piano owes a great deal to the efforts of George Shearing who, in the early fifties, had released several books containing the piano transcriptions of the tunes he had performed and recorded with his famous George Shearing Quintet. Denny was one of the lounge musicians who bought those books and used some of their techniques when he had a trio early in his career.

There is also the time-honored Hammond organ, which took the otherworldly charm of church serenades into hotel lounges and supper clubs where the ice of juleps counterpoints the dice at crap tables. Don Baker and his trio had played at Las Vegas clubs with his Hammond, accompanied by celestes, drums, and piano for sparkling arrangements of such titles as "Poinciana," "Shangri-La," and "Caravan." The cover to his Capitol album *Cocktail Hammond* depicts him at his keyboards, surrounded by an array of beautiful blondes in tight black cocktail dresses, brandishing Martinis and coy looks.

Among the most celebrated pop-music Hammond wizards is Lenny Dee, who began playing organ at several swanky hotels in the South and elevated his career as a regular at the Plantation Club in Nashville. Through the years, Dee released many albums covering sixties and seventies favorites and was a standard contributor to the late and lamented "Beautiful Music" radio programs. He would also play at his nightclub in St. Petersburg, Florida, Lenny Dee's Den. There he would provide electronic melodies, lovely and haunting enough to make a song like "Moonlight Cocktail" invite possible connections between liquor and lycanthropy.

Transition Bars and Cocktail Widows

Drinking places when located in less residential or in suspect parts of town have an inverted charm precisely because they are impermanent. Transition bars, usually in the vicinity of bus terminals, train depots, and airports, are intended to serve people on the move. By their very nature, transition bars bring out the more peculiar character angles that always surface when people are *between* destinations. With names like Tube Bar, Terminal Bar, or Way Station, transition bars suggest rootlessness or ill repute and usually bear none of the standard lounge's elaborate settings. Still, they offer the same modus operandi of packaged time.

Commuters can always stop at a transition bar to make the span between the 5:22 and the 6:09 go by faster, though for some it can become an eternity. To enter a transition bar is to enter limbo, an ephemeral interval that discourages attachments yet goads the lonely. And what types are attracted to such places? Out-of-town travelers who come only once; everyday commuters or regulars who just need a place to hang out between connections; working men and women seeking a neutral outpost between the job and the home; or the desperate who are either unemployed or retired, tottering on their stools and reading false promises in each new face.

A *cocktail widow* is an enduring fixture at transition bars, although she can materialize in any lounge. She might seem another lonely woman left standing at the brass rail, searching for a soul in the eyes of passing men she will never have. She shows up in many forties and fifties movies, where she sits around like a gaping void, waiting for some vague sense of community but always eliciting trouble. In the 1944 murder mystery *Phantom Lady,* her fiancé passed away, so she sits alone at a bar and grill. She is the unwitting catalyst for disaster when a man with wife problems comes into the bar and befriends the woman out of desperation. After taking her to the theater and saying good-bye at the very pub where he found her, he returns home to find his wife murdered and is later jailed as the suspect. Once a friend finally tracks the cocktail widow down to help prove the man's whereabouts when the killing occurred, she is too dejected and insane to remember what happened.

In a 1958 *Playboy* article, Philip Wylie provided a caricature of the modern, "untamable" woman holding "a drink in one hand and some books in the other." The narrator of Wylie's semi-autobiographical novel *Opus 21* learns he has a cancerous node in his throat and decides to live out his final days to their fullest by taking residence in a swanky New York City hotel. At one point, he goes to the hotel bar and introduces himself to a beautiful woman twirling her "amber" cocktail and reading the Kinsey report. In Wylie's eyes: "She had been packaged in the best fashion of the richest and most powerful culture of the twentieth century. . . . In representing the highest peak of what is called civilization she presented the least sensitive arrangement of what is called human." The novel's overriding sentiment is that "booze and broads, taken as a platter combination and not à la carte, are more threatening than pleasurable."

Victor "Trader Vic" Bergeron, in his *Bartender's Guide,* alludes to cocktail widows in a chapter called "People That Bartenders Don't Like": "You can't miss the gal who gets chummy with every unattached male in the place. She is most likely a tramp and probably soliciting." Despite Bergeron's contempt, cocktail widows are right to assume that transition bars give their lingering looks an air of legitimacy. After all, she could really be waiting for her train.

But chances are she is no different from everyone else in the place, going nowhere but pretending to be "just passing through."

Transition bars abroad can trap isolated tourists with the grisliest of fates. Protagonist Karen Stone, in the film version of Tennessee Williams's novella *The Roman Spring of Mrs. Stone,* drifts into a cavernous nightclub. To complement the fright masks and candlelight, Cleo Laine sings softly with an aimless stare. Mrs. Stone's Negroni* symbolizes her state of mind, a place Williams describes as "a universe of turbulently rushing fluids and vapors." Its gin cradled in sweet vermouth aids her desire to drift out of middle-aged servitude into the arms of gigolos, yet the Campari adds a bitter undertaste that prepares her for a violent end. Can the next wayward turn into the Terminal Inn make us foreigners in our own lands? Strangers to those we once took for granted as banal?

Caligari's Bar and Grill

Ever walk into a bar that adjusts to your dark mood? Have you ever seen your mind's recesses reflected back in the eerie lights and long, tilted corridors branching out into

---

*The bitter-sweet Negroni is of European origin but has a tenuous American link, if only because of its original name. Sometime during the 1920s, Count Camillo Negroni, a prominent Florentine aristocrat, supposedly visited Italy's Casoni Bar and asked the bartender for an "Americano," consisting of equal parts Campari, sweet vermouth, and gin. The count liked it so much and ordered it so many times, and at so many places, that the drink eventually assumed his identity.

mysterious side rooms? Once in a while, the lounge connoisseur can encounter such special places with designs suggesting amusement park "dark rides."

In Mickey Spillane's novel *Vengeance Is Mine,* Mike Hammer enters a New York establishment called the Bowery Inn. Beyond "half-boarded-up windows, flyspecked beer signs, and an outward appearance of something long ago gone to seed," he encounters a "fancy chrome-trimmed bar" and "plush-lined seats" with a spotlight on "a completely naked woman doing a strip tease in reverse."

In no time, Hammer traverses a fun house path of doors within doors. They at last lead to a casino done up to look "like an old-fashioned Western gambling hall" that harbors shifty-eyed denizens and women who turn into men. It turns out to be a scam headquarters where pretty girls entice philandering husbands who are then photographed and blackmailed. Spillane's surreal fifties excursions into dangerous drinking dens address the anxieties of GIs returning to a changed America. Spillane, himself a former Air Force fighter pilot and cadet instructor, seems familiar and oddly enamored with these secret rooms and onion-skin selves that get more abstruse with each peeled layer.

Few literary descriptions of cocktail lounges gone amok are as devastating and alluring as Fritz Leiber's in his science-fiction novel *The Sinful Ones.* Its protagonist discovers that the world is literally inhabited by clockwork automatons. All around him, life assumes a "synthetic, movie-and-radio shaped nature" amid the gazes of billboard advertisements, deceptive clocks, and blinking neon. The only other person who sees through the façade is a woman with whom he, at one point, escapes into a cocktail lounge called Goldie's Casablanca. But there is no way out. The lounge's menagerie of "horse-faced" bartenders in white coats, "violently shaking" silver cylinders, fast-talking patrons, and a manic pianist crystallize into a "bacchanal shrunk to a precalculated and profit-motivated booze-fest under the direction of a Pan who'd gone all to watery flesh and been hitting the dope for two thousand years."

But one person's den of iniquity is another's con-sumer utopia. The primary purpose of lounges, after all, is to make people experience all the comforts of home that even homes cannot provide. Architect Hugh Hardy (who redesigned New York's famed Rainbow Room in the late 1980s) summarizes a prevailing attitude among many de-signers that lounges, like butcher sections in supermarkets, should make the flesh look appetizing: "You have to give people the kind of creature comforts to make them feel they're in a special place. . . . We used a palette that was very dark so that at night the faces and the clothes stand out. We never use strong colors because then people won't look good to each other. And if they don't look good to each other, they spend less."

Cocktail Couple. By the fifties, cocktails became a talisman for urban so-phisticates on the move. Even the proximity of a neon "Cocktails" sign en-couraged "good life" enthusiasts to evolve into the packaged personalities which we can still hope to become in moments of optimism. (Michael Ochs Archives, Venice, Calif.)

8

Sirens of the Cold War
(The Cocktail Chanteuse)

What happens . . . when it never comes the way you want it?
Like music that never reaches a pitch? What do you do? Go
on singing songs and drinking Ramos Gin Fizzes?

—Lizabeth Scott, *Dead Reckoning*

Draped across pianos, often in pouty poses and tight black dresses, they sang of lovemaking, hearts breaking, and sweet revenge. These were cocktail sirens, urban mermaids brewed from the ice Cold War and the image vats of Hollywood and Madison Avenue.

Long before Peggy Lee breathed her husky but sultry "Fever" into the home hi-fi or the lamé-draped Abbe Lane sang and danced the cha-cha at Ciro's, cocktail sirens had their first true incarnation in Hollywood's film noir. Lauren Bacall, for one, had played a nightclub seductress who wooed the tough but psychologically vulnerable Bogart.

An even more notable example is a Bacall substitute, actress Lizabeth Scott, who plays mystery blonde Coral Chandler in the 1946 postwar mystery *Dead Reckoning*.

When she takes to the stage to sing "Either It's Love or It Isn't," Bogart (as ex-GI-turned-sleuth Rip Murdock) gets taken not only by her ambiguous message but by an intrigue involving his best friend's murder. In this role, Scott supplies all of the cocktail siren's essential ingredients, as varied and as deceptively sweet as the Ramos Gin Fizzes she drinks between performances at the film's Sanctuary Club. The powdered-sugar and egg-whites smile, the orange-flower hairstyle and creamy dress, the lemon-lime sarcasm, and the cold gin interior are all vigorously shaken into a spectacle rivaling Salome's dance of the seven veils.

The cocktail siren often has an advantage: When singing her lovelorn tunes to the gullible gumshoe, she has the option of falling back on the excuse that it was all just an act. The 1952 psychological thriller *Don't Bother to Knock* presents the ironic contrast between a cocktail siren's persona on and off the stage. The movie starts in a swanky New York hotel, with Anne Bancroft moping at a bar and complaining to the bartender about her insensitive boyfriend. Suddenly the lights dim, she makes a 180-degree turn on her barstool, holds up a microphone, puts on a happy face in the glare of a spotlight, and begins singing an upbeat tune. She does not miss a beat through this, one of many nightly appearances at the Western-themed Round-Up Room, unaware that an emotionally disturbed woman (played by Marilyn Monroe) will soon attempt a murder in one of the hotel's suites.

In the recording studio, the cocktail siren's Hollywood image became equally complicated. Her songs, as

Abbe Lane at Ciro's. Ciro's was among the "fabulous" nightclubs where the Hollywood elite held their civic rituals. Posing outside the club to promote her shows, Abbe Lane takes on the role of Tinseltown's pagan goddess: a human cocktail shaker. She also poses a metaphysical riddle that someone experiencing the neural nudge of a good drink could appreciate: Is the foreground Abbe the "real" Abbe? Or merely the two-dimensional likeness of infinite Abbes that multiply beyond the camera? (Michael Ochs Archives, Venice, Calif.)

well as her calculated poses on album covers, made her both manipulative and vulnerable. She truly came into her own by the mid-fifties when women were stereotyped as either the suburban hausfrau (June Cleaver) or the manicured tart (Jayne Mansfield). As a singer of songs and a role model, a siren had to satisfy the fantasies of gray-flannel suitors who charmed their wives with luxury appliances and kept their mistresses in diamonds.

Cocktail siren psychology owes some debt to both the distiller and print media industries for finally allowing women to appear in liquor ads. In the past, advertisements for whiskey were usually the domain of Lord Calvert–style patriarchs: natty suits and hegemonic hauteur. Then, with the postwar increase in vodka sales and the marketing savvy behind such inventions as the Moscow Mule and the Bloody Mary, companies like Smirnoff began to showcase sultry and seductive vixens who were foxy yet lovable enough to convince a Soviet-wary public it was okay to indulge in a Communist export.

Julie London emerged as the consummate cocktail siren. Movie star, club performer, recording artist, and occasional television personality, she was also the perfect physical type for conveying aerodynamic glamour in the new age of mass-produced Frigidaires and televisions. She was a blend of Dionysian flesh and Detroit steel, streamlined car and cocktail shaker combined. Her cool, sleek, and supple contours, cobalt blue eyes, and high-tech vocals satisfied America's fascination for what Marshall McLuhan called "the assembly-line goddess."

Born Julie Peck on September 26, 1926, in Santa Rosa, California, Julie London literally *rose* to stardom as an elevator operator at a Hollywood department store, where she was talent-scouted by agent Sue Carol (Alan Ladd's wife). Her first role was opposite Buster Crabbe in the 1944 low-budget adventure movie *Nabonga,* playing a jungle waif in the African wild with a cache of stolen jewels and a gorilla companion. Not until her early fifties divorce from Cold War–enthusiast Jack Webb did she opt for a singing career.

While dating, Julie sang "Little Girl Blue" to songwriter and husband-to-be Bobby Troup who, in turn, promptly got her a contract with Bethlehem Records for a breathy four-song demo backed by his own combo. Once they married in 1954, Julie got her first "live" exposure at Johnny Walsh's 881 Club in Los Angeles. Without bigband roots, Julie preferred these foggy evening settings, which promised intimacy yet always sent customers home with halfhearted dreams left behind in half-empty glasses.

Troup cut a deal with Si Waronker of Liberty Records in 1955 to record *Julie Is Her Name,* her first album, which also featured the label's then highly touted "Spectra-Sonic-Sound." Ray Leatherwood's wandering bass, Barney Kessel's oozing guitar, and an occasional echo delay on songs like "Laura" and her one big hit, "Cry Me a River," allowed record buyers to recapture the smoky magic of the 881 Club surroundings in their living rooms.

If Russ Columbo supplied the vocal vermouth, Julie was the gin or vodka that tempered torch songs to a flickering propane blue. Hers was the witchy allure that stuck enough in people's minds through the decades to influence Michelle Pfeiffer, who as Susie Diamond in *The Fabulous Baker Boys*, made a noble attempt to be just as provocative and spooky by performing "Makin' Whoopee" while undulating over Jeff Bridges's lounge piano.

Julie London's music also incited a fresh repertoire of amorous responses, making romance more a matter of environment than emotion. Many of her songs are less about passion than about its accoutrements: the jewels, the satin sheets, the colognes, the afteroffice dinners, and, best of all, the cocktail interlude when many pecuniary deals are forged. For the cover of her 1961 album, *Whatever Julie Wants,* Julie had to have special armed security men stand guard as she posed beside almost $750,000 worth of furs, jewels, and piles of paper money. A UPI press photo of the event reveals an empty champagne glass in the foreground—the insatiable Fury's talisman.

In the liner notes to *Julie Is Her Name,* Hollywood screenwriter Richard Breen claims: "If there must be definition, she is less the gaudy nightingale and more the bird of passage. A bird of passage is one that sings in a lost corner of the garden." The anonymous notes to her second album, *Lonely Girl,* go further: "There's an appealing loneliness in Julie. She has a way of getting out on a plane all by herself where no one can reach her."

Part of Julie's distancing effect was the way she sucessfully distilled the blues into chilled mood melodies, renouncing the assumption that torch songs require a wail or a groan. Defending her refusal to be just another hand-wringing torch singer, she once flatly stated: "I can belt songs out, but I don't like them that way."

Julie's rejection of "authentic" passion explains the circumstances behind her most famous recording, "Cry Me a River." Composer Arthur Hamilton, whom she had befriended at Hollywood Professional School, wrote the song for Ella Fitzgerald to sing in Jack Webb's 1955 film *Pete Kelly's Blues*. With Julie's interpretation, the would-be "soulful" version became as ectoplasmic as the apparition she portrays a year later in Frank Tashlin's *The Girl Can't Help It,* when she sings it to a love-smitten and intoxicated Tom Ewell, haunting him from room to room.

As an actress, Julie's best screen moments are liquor-laced. In *The Fat Man* (based on one of Dashiell Hammett's radio creations), which RKO studios released in 1951, Julie plays a girl adrift in the big city, abandoned by the man of her dreams (who turns out to be a vagrant criminal played by a very young Rock Hudson). But lest we mistake her character for a naif, the camera introduces her to us by lasciviously moving up her body as she sits at a bar holding a cigarette and meditating beside her drink. *The Voice in the Mirror* (1958), whose title song she co-composed, casts her as the dutiful wife fighting her chronic drinker husband's excesses. As a nightclub singer in *The George Raft Story* (1961), she bids her ex-gangster-turned-actor boyfriend farewell with a tart rendition of "What Can I Say After I Say I'm Sorry?"

Her best performance was undoubtedly in the 1954

movie *The Great Man*, directed by and starring Jose Ferrer as a wary journalist desperately trying to write a positive obit for a recently deceased and highly execrable broadcasting magnate. In one key scene, Julie appears as nightclub singer Carol Larson, who is also the deceased's former "kept" girlfriend. As Ferrer coaxes her to recount how she had been corrupted, emotionally imprisoned, beaten, and finally rejected, Julie's character prowls around her apartment, pouring scotch, progressively staggering and slurring her words. She suddenly starts singing along when, by some pie-eyed coincidence, her real-life recording of "The Meaning of the Blues" spews out of the radio.

Julie London's voice is so perfect for the drinking mood that she can incite thirst simply by humming a wordless *doo-doo-dah-doo* to the instrumental "Hot Toddy" or floating through André Previn's orchestral accompaniment on "One for My Baby," a song Sinatra made popular about the lyrical lamentations of a bartender and the customer whose feet are planted firmly on the brass rail but whose heart dissolves into the glass. In "Pousse Café," she knows that since "an aperitif can't bring relief," she will make "a toast to a dream" while contemplating this layered liqueur that, like her heart, has three parts. "Something Cool" transports her to an exotic summer locale where she can blame her hormonal urges on the heat while savoring an icy tonic.

Julie's more whimsical side comes out when she does Cole Porter's "Make It Another Old Fashioned, Please." This song got its first exposure through Ethel Merman

Julie London. As Julie London looks toward heaven, she thanks her muse for a singing voice as refined and distilled as the elixir in her glass. Julie's melodic mixture of after-hours guitars, bedroom saxophones, and lush violins complements a slow-motion delivery that evokes Salvador Dalí's melting clocks. The great Surrealist himself once stated that a good drink should "linger awhile in the heady orifice to be carried to every membrane of memory and dream." But Julie does him one better on her version of the J. Fred Coots–Haven Gillespie tune "You Go to My Head." Here, falling in love becomes synonymous with the circuitous route that champagne bubbles take before they finally make their welcomed revolutions around the brain. (Michael Ochs Archives, Venice, Calif.)

when she played a brassy nightclub singer in the musical *Panama Hattie,* but Julie's interpretation is unadulterated deadpan. Another cry-into-your-scotch-and-seltzer melody is "Well, Sir," which Troup wrote for her *London by Night* album. It is about a woman who goes into a "lonely bar" and claims not to "feel much like talking" but at the slightest provocation lapses into a sob.

In 1962, Julie released *Love on the Rocks,* one of her most intriguing "themed" albums about the backwash of romances past. The album's title song conjures a darkly romantic recipe that includes "a jigger of lying," "some bitters for crying," and "a dash of lost dreams." While many other singers have handled and reinterpreted this and other liquor-related songs, Julie's distilled style makes the term "cocktail singer" a definitive one. When Julie London sings, you can taste the Martini!

9

Toasting the Noble Neurotic

Civilization begins with distillation.
—William Faulkner

Rootless, overanxious, understimulated, compulsive, agoraphobic, prone to melancholy, out of touch with what religion and social science call "true" passion, nostalgic about a nonexistent past and uncertain about the future—these, conventional wisdom dictates, are the traits of people in deep trouble. But, from a wider view, they are qualities of distinction, possessed by men and women who have come to terms with modern life's tragicomic cocktail drama.

Welcome to the world of the Noble Neurotic, a proud though nerve-racking place that has captured the imaginations and secret destinies of Americans of many walks, shades, and persuasions. The Noble Neurotic is the star in an ultracivilized existence that offers precious moments of adventure, of visionary quests, of transitory fellowship illuminated by artificial lights and distilled dreams.

If the wilderness satisfied Rousseau's noble savage, cocktail surroundings are the Noble Neurotic's domain. The term *neurotic* may still carry an antiquated yet official baggage of negativism, but the Noble Neurotic is a cocktail hero supreme who elevates "neuroticism" from a pathology to a positive and life-affirming manifesto.

Noble Neurotics are vexed yet inspired by what social anthropologist Desmond Morris once described as the "Stimulus Struggle." Scrubbed up, manicured, and divorced from a hunter-gatherer past, they nonetheless retain vestiges of the same emotional nemeses that dogged frontiersmen and intrepid warriors. Much like caged animals, Noble Neurotics compensate for their inescapable state of man-made incarceration by devising an elaborate coping mechanism. In this case, the substitutes include compulsive hobbies, sexual fetishes, and a great deal of ritual eating and drinking.

Neurosis became a noble avocation sometime after World War II. Soldiers came back to a different America that was soon changed by media manipulations that had helped to redefine human personality. The urban leisure drinker was so prevalent that it seemed pathological *not* to have a cocktail. The 1950 movie *The Big Hangover* captures the returning G.I.'s psychological adjustment. Van Johnson is an ex-soldier who, during service, was wounded and sent to a monastery in the French Alps. After being trapped for fourteen hours inside its cellar during an air-raid, he is almost drowned when barrels of hundred-year-old brandy explode all around him. He comes back to the States with what a medical journal calls "the biggest hangover in medical science" and experiences a total-recall intoxication when imbibing even a drop of liquor.

The Big Hangover is a satire on what happens to someone who cannot drink in an environment where drinking is not just a means of escape or recreation but a form of social decorum. For the postwar consumer, cocktail time was a solidifying ritual that (despite the persistent bad press that alcohol leads to social unrest) brought stability to a world that was revamping all of its past mores.

For many fifties cocktail-party habitués, the mere act of seeing a psychiatrist held cachet. There were even cocktail characters emerging in the media such as comedian Ernie Kovacs's cross-eyed Percy Dovetonsils who lisps his poetry while sipping his Martini, or that less enviable figure appearing in the film *Breakfast at Tiffany's* who, at Holly Golightly's cocktail party, holds a drink while laughing with and at herself in the mirror one moment and crying the next.

By the fifties, it was obvious that somewhere between the defunct individualism implied by the Protestant ethic and the evolving bureaucracy lay a maladjusted soul awaiting some form of emotional and spiritual completion. William H. Whyte Jr.'s study *The Organization Man* points out how the executive character emerging after World War II is caught between the heartfelt world of his family, friends, and relatives and the glacial demands of a job that saps more and more of his time. The cocktail bar, whether built inside the office or waiting outside just around the corner, was the way station where fellow compulsives could either formalize their thoughts or, at times, even free-associate. J. Pierrepont Finch, the antihero in Frank Loesser's musical *How to Succeed in Business (Without Really Trying),* climbs from window washer to a top adman at the Worldwide Wicket Company. At the crest of his ambitions, he gazes into the executive washroom mirror to sing about how "making it" has "the slam bang tang reminiscent of gin and vermouth."

Writing about some postwar fiction, William H. Whyte Jr. points out how some stories tended to moralize about this situation: "The entrepreneur, as many see him, is a selfish type motivated by greed, and he is, furthermore, unhappy. The bigtime operator as sketched in fiction eventually so loses stomach for enterprise, forsakes '21,' El Morocco, and the boss's wife and heads for the country."

Sloan Wilson's novel *The Man in the Gray Flannel Suit* is about Tom Rath, an ex-Army paratrooper who seeks a job at a public-relations firm, with the goal of buying "a more expensive house and a better brand of gin." Rath, however, proves to be more of a drone than a doer, eventually choosing the less distinguished and pressured life of a generic nine-to-fiver. The novel's true Noble Neurotic is Rath's boss Ralph Hopkins, the head of United Broadcasting Company, who is beleaguered by a failed marriage, a delinquent eighteen-year-old daughter who "lives in nightclubs," and a tendency to be melancholy. Imprisoned in his luxurious office high rise, he somehow finds momentary solace in his full bar and an ironic pet project for the promotion of mental health.

Jack London's novel *Burning Daylight* had already made similar analogies between the cocktail-loving executive and a kind of emotional incarceration that comes naturally with the territory. Years later, director Nicolas Roeg's film *The Man Who Fell to Earth* would portray David Bowie as an alleged space alien who markets a series of patents to make himself a multimillionaire head of World Enterprises. The Martini comes to symbolize America's corporate carrot when his fondness for gin parallels his ascent on the cosmic elevator to success. Along the way he is captured by rivals and placed in maximum-security luxury, in which each morning he must face a waiter who wheels a portable ice-box along corridors of period furniture and discarded art objects to serve up a "not too cold" Martini.

The Martini, the stiletto heel of cocktails, is among the Noble Neurotic's most treasured props. Its stem is so far off its surface that it forces its holder into a contrived posture. In some respects, it could be the best partition between man and the feral world. At one point in their novel *Illuminatus!,* authors Robert Shea and Robert Anton Wilson stretch the Martini as a metaphor for capitalist excess much further. Here, perverse executives dream up the concept of a "plastic nude martini," to be served out of nonbiodegradable "transparent plastic bags" in the shape of naked women as a celebration of corporate, sexual, and environmental exploitation.

Further evidence of the Martini's role as neurotic contrivance is its past use in ersatz manhood rituals. An example is the hazing rite at Harvard's Owl Club, in which a group of undergraduate fraternity brothers use a "Martini ritual" to break in newcomers. After chugging several drinks in full public view, the initiates are blindfolded and commanded to crawl through several obstacles until they, if lucky, finally wander into the private "members only" rooms.

A sixties ad for Martini & Rossi's Imported Vermouth has a man in a safari suit sitting proudly beside his caged female. The ad reads: ". . . for cocktails that purr. Sweet for captivating Manhattans, Extra dry for Martinis. Try it in your cage." The ad suggests a moral: There is nothing more nobly neurotic than pretending to be Tarzan in a land of theme parks. Part of the Noble Neurotic's charm is his or her ability to imagine they have entered the great unknown via television or CinemaScope. Actor Tom Ewell plays that part flawlessly in the 1955 movie *The Seven Year Itch,* as a hen-pecked fifties husband who is prone to sexual wanderlust when his wife and child go out of town. As he fixes Marilyn Monroe a Tom Collins, he blathers on about "the labyrinth of the human mind" where "under this thin veneer of civilization we're all savages; man, woman—hopelessly enmeshed."

Ewell's character is the prototype of many men who were coming to terms with a new American identity. *The Seven Year Itch* was released in 1955, that pivotal year when rock and roll was becoming a household word and the post-

The Atomic Drinker. The Nuclear Age had changed drinking. A concoction called the "Atomic Cocktail" was a short-lived novelty fad, but the nightmarish associations of the atom bomb, Cold War paranoia, and the growing awareness of challenged sexual roles turned some drinking places into dens of confusion and intrigue. Artist Jana Christy's rendering of "The Atomic Drinker" suggests that today's most urbane men and women can still fall prey to psychic vampires and sinister Shriners. A man gazes into his radioactive drink, flanked by his shadow woman and grazed by a prevailing though unseen male bent on a combination of sabotage and sexual favors. (Cover of "Very Vicky" comic book, Issue 5, by Jana Christy, © 1994 Jana Christy, P.O. Box 383286, Cambridge, Mass. 02238)

war Organization Man was an official figurehead of our culture. We had won and survived two world wars, exploded the first atomic bomb, synthesized plastic, had the first official sex change, and, in the mix, had earned the prestige of being the Earth's model cocktail consumers.

The notion of liquor lubricating the wheels of free enterprise runs parallel with the theory that many of our prized writers have about their own work output. Tom Dardis notes, in his cautionary book *The Thirsty Muse,* that five of the seven Americans to receive the Nobel Prize for literature, including Ernest Hemingway, William Faulkner, and Eugene O'Neill, were heavy drinkers. They had inadvertently created a more complex character type: the literary visionary who resorts to liquor to liberate ideas that sobriety otherwise suppresses.

Hemingway was among the prime proponents of alcohol's idea-enhancing properties, convinced that the distillates allow writers their dream: to see the world as a pure verbal abstraction divorced from affect. Psychologists would later distort this idea by deeming excessive and logically disconnected chatter in neurological patients "cocktail party syndrome." But for most creative thinkers/drinkers, cocktail time brings on a beneficial *alcolalia.*

J. D. Salinger, in his novel *The Catcher in the Rye,* shows how cocktail time is just as important for an adolescent's rite of passage as it is for the rigors of adult life. The story's narrator, the eminently troubled Holden Caulfield, is a precocious minor who often wanders into cocktail lounges. Due to his ungainly height and prematurely graying crew cut, he is usually able to pass himself off as an adult. On one occasion, Caulfield visits the Wicker Bar at New York's Seton Hotel. He downs scotch-and-sodas before meeting up with an old friend who was once his high school student adviser but now acts as an unofficial sex informer. The cocktail lounge serves as the ideal setting in which to fill this chronically malcontented boy with chatter about the habits of sheep lovers, lesbians, and panty fetishists, as well as the kinky proclivities of some movie stars.

The fact that something as contrived and effete as the cocktail was used to buttress Madison Avenue images of manhood was an irony not lost on many. In the mounting arena of cocktail types populating movies and lounges alike, machos and fairies no longer became warring contrasts, but desperadoes catfighting for a niche on the Kinsey continuum.

Still others, like socialist Lionel Tiger, took a less ironic approach. His book *Men in Groups,* a late-sixties attempt to rectify a sneaking suspicion that "maleness" was being threatened, mentions the importance of drink in masculine bonding. He even suggests that the Scandinavian salute "Skoal" may be derived from "skull," the vessel from which primitives drank the blood of their human prey.

Others like Hugh Hefner were much more satirical and savvy, turning the virility cult into highly profitable variations on male camp. Instead of drinking from skulls, the doyens of cool posing beside their "bunnies" in the pages of *Playboy* usually held their cocktails in vessels of svelte crystal. By 1965, Hefner could flaunt reports that 86.9

percent of *Playboy*'s subscriber households served some kind of alcoholic beverage, a figure that at the time outranked those of all other magazines. To show he shared the same values as his readers, Hefner often displayed the consummate cocktail lounge inside his seventy-room Playboy mansion. It included what Hefner once referred to as a "self-contained private world" with a CinemaScope living room, state-of-the-art stereo, and swimming pool replete with an underwater bar.

Again, the constant reminder of sex and religion (particularly Catholicism) lends a mythological legitimacy to drinking. Eugene O'Neill offers a portrait of a psychosexually and spiritually famished family in *A Long Day's Journey into Night.* Here a drug-addict mother (and former nun) struts about the house in a metaphysical delirium. The father and his two sons hover around bottles of whiskey while contemplating a "saint's vision of beatitude." But for them the bottle can only provide a glimpse of eternity. As nobly as possible, they face the neurotic's conundrum: The moment they think they have reached eternity, they panic and pull back. Once again, in that safe region of frustrated needs and outmoded beliefs, Noble Neurotics at least have the resourcefulness to sit back and watch as "the hand lets the veil fall, and you're alone, lost in the fog again."

10

The Olive in the Hourglass

Between the dark and the daylight,
When the night is beginning to lower,
Comes a pause in the day's occupations,
That is known as the Children's Hour.
　　　—Henry Wadsworth Longfellow,
　　　　　　The Children's Hour

Alcohol makes a clock stand still.
　　　—Gordon Jenkins,
　　　　　Seven Dreams

 The cocktail glass is the top half of the hourglass, the part reminding us of minutes remaining and draining.

Cocktail hour is witching hour, when devils and angels chaperon each sip and gloat over our awkward submission to dusk.

Cocktail time is the twilight zone between day and night, when egos disrobe and vampires prepare to dine.

The setting sun and rising moon can play havoc with heartbeat and metabolism. Birds are known to screech in near panic, mammals to alter their mating and eating patterns. Human navigation, hormonal responses, and reasoning powers also vary as solar intensity wanes. This makes the best cocktail parties a skillful orchestration of soft lights and sweet music with nature's tidal shifts.

Why dusk has become the cocktail party convention is fraught with contradictions. On one hand, it is a time of reprieve from the workaday demands that speed up metabolism and tax concentration; on the other, it is the part of the day most open to angst. One experiment determined that the heart rates of people who prefer evening usually peak between 5:00 and 6:30 P.M. Between 6:30 and 8:30 P.M., long-term memory skills may sharpen, but alcohol is most intoxicating and takes longest to filter through the liver at around 7 P.M. than at any other time.

A 1986 Pepperdine University study investigated the relationship between circadian rhythms and personality. Researchers presented the Maudsley Personality Inventory, along with a "Morningness-Eveningness Questionnaire," to 116 college students with ages ranging from twenty to sixty-four years. The results indicated that evening types are more prone than morning types to pessimism and "neuroticism."

Circadian rhythms, based on how the brain responds to light, may explain why the human desire for cocktail time's artificial darkness parallels the sandhopper's automatic dash for the sea at the first hint of moonlight. Author J. G. Ballard explores this link between animal instincts, human compulsion, and cocktails at dusk in his short story "The Delta at Sunset." Camping outside an ancient Toltec city, an ailing archaeologist gets relief from his constant fevers only when he sits outside his tent at sunset. He sips

whiskey sodas and watches the nightly brigade of interlocking snakes wriggle toward the beaches.

Notwithstanding the Pavlovian slaver that some people spew when the words "cocktail time" are spoken, the
cocktail hour is a ceremonial disunion of man from beast.
Bernard DeVoto's *The Hour* (first published in 1948) describes cocktail time as "the violet hour" that "marks the
lifeward turn. The heart wakens from coma and its dys-
pnea dens. Its strengthening pulse is to cross over into
campground, to believe that the world has not been altogether lost or, if lost, then not altogether in vain."

Behind its hedonistic and trivial veneer, cocktail time
masks a deeper mysticism. By 6:00 P.M., a subtler (transcendent or threatening) counterenergy takes over, connecting
bottled spirits to the spirit world. Richard Cavendish states
in *The Black Arts:* "Some medieval alchemists thought that
alcohol was a form of the quintessence, the pure fifth ele-
ment of which the heavens are made." Church of Satan
founder Anton LaVey claims, "The best thing about any
day is its gentle lapse into night, the dark mantle whence all
secrets evolve."

T. S. Eliot's *The Cocktail Party* cloaks the ritual in
priestly garments. Here, "the violet hour" is a secular answer to the Roman Catholic confession and mass. Eliot's
play culled many literary influences: Greek mythology, a
then fashionable existentialism, as well as middlebrow
dramas about adultery and passion that predate soap op-
eras. *The Cocktail Party* considers how even the most "in-
dulgent" occurrences bear occult ciphers and potential

miracles. Literary critic D. E. Jones claims: "The cocktail party can be the secular counterpart of the Communion Service if given in the right spirit, the tidbits and the short drinks the equivalent of bread and wine. The play is almost a piece of metaphysical wit in its discovery of analogy in unlikely places."

For Eliot, the cocktail party is a catalyst for social and marital cures. Two couples in a love quadrangle find salvation by toasting the hearth and heeding the cryptic advice of an "Uninvited Guest" who turns out to be a psychiatrist. The main character, after cheating on his wife and finding out he does not really love the other woman, experiences a "loss of personality": He can no longer perceive himself "through the eyes of other people." But the psychiatrist heals by performing a sacrament, adding a drop of water to his glass of gin to trigger a chain of divine reactions that reunites the couple, even though they will never truly understand each other.

First shown in 1949, *The Cocktail Party* played havoc with British minds before it reached America. Eliot, the American expatriate and WASP-turned-Catholic, wanted to present the spiritual options left to London's fashionable crowd, which was undergoing its own postwar cocktail renaissance. After all, it was Winston Churchill who once celebrated his fondness of scotch with a painting called *Bottlescape* and claimed, "The use of intoxicants is one of the distinguishing marks of the higher types and races of humanity."

P. G. Wodehouse had a more traditionally British prejudice against cocktail parties. His 1950 novel *Cocktail*

Time is about a stodgy barrister and Parliament aspirant who gets hit on the head with a brazil nut. Though a fellow lord threw it as a joke, the barrister concludes it is the work of some ill-bred, new-generation hooligan bedeviled by America's influential bad manners. To let off steam, he pens a novel called *Cocktail Time,* relegating authorial credit to his nephew to avoid scandal. The book turns out to be a success with a movie deal in the works. The barrister soon forfeits his moral grandeur when he scrambles to retrieve a document that proves him the true scribe.

Even in America, home of the Manhattan and the Highball, cocktail time had its fair share of critics. Composer Gordon Jenkins recorded a narrative album called *Seven Dreams* that saunters through a series of fantasies about human rites of passage. One of them is a cocktail party, a ritual Jenkins's narrator describes as "modern society's alcoholic refuge for the insecure." It is a place where aspiring personalities and social clowns play mind games with one another. In 1957, composer Harry Partch produced a dance satire (in his words "a psychological striptease") called *The Bewitched.* Lampooning our ultra-civilized preference for intellect over instinct, he includes one apocalyptic and noisy interlude entitled "The Cognoscenti Are Plunged into a Demonic Descent While at Cocktails."

It was this often misguided fear and loathing of middle-class fifties mores that perhaps inspired journalist C. B. Palmer's 1952 article "The Consummately Dry Martini," in which he deems such cocktails a fetish unique to "the Numb (or Glazed) Fifties." But it was the fifties cocktail and its many attendant parties that most likely juiced up the high-tech leisure and information culture many Americans and Western Europeans take for granted today.

During the fifties and early sixties, Martinis in particular soothed the "Organization Man" as he contemplated the technological paradox that produced the atom bomb yet raised standards of living. Like the Protestant work ethic, Martinis were clean, severe, and bracing; like a Roman Catholic mass, they offered short-term ethereal rapture fraught with symbolism.

The perfect Martini represented both status and a common ethos for perfection. Once William Powell applied his vermouth with a dropper in *The Thin Man,* a cottage industry of Martini implements started evolving. James Bond, that model of Anglo-American restraint and cool machismo, must have raised eyebrows when in the film *Dr. No,* he ordered his Martini "shaken, not stirred." After all, many still entertained the superstition that gin (or vodka) could be "bruised." The Gibson did not damage the liquor but it left out an essential Martini component. Artist Charles Dana Gibson (inventor of the Gibson Girl) had the drink named after him at his favorite New York club, The Players, when he was served a Martini with two white pearl onions because the customary olives were out of stock.

In 1949, M. F. K. Fisher wrote in the *Atlantic Monthly* that "a well-made Martini or Gibson, correctly chilled and nicely served, has been more often my true friend than any two-legged creature." The Martini offered reassurance but could also shake social foundations. "A woman with six

Martinis can ruin a city," says a character in the film *The Big Knife,* discussing how the lethal combination of juniper juices and wry conversation makes people dispense privileged information. The Martini can also be an invitation to infidelity, as demonstrated in the 1963 movie *Wives and Lovers.* Janet Leigh plays a wifely paragon of virtue who talks friends out of a night at the "21" club to join her and husband (Van Johnson) for a private cocktail party at their new Connecticut home. Jeremy Slate plays the dashing young actor friend who flaunts all manly muscle while mixing Leigh his special dry vodka Martini with only an "essence of vermouth." Leigh becomes an instant adulteress after her first sip.

Like the denizens of T. S. Eliot's cocktail party, movie characters and viewers alike had tried (and continue trying) to live out the middle-class dream despite twinges of self-doubt; what David Riesman in his 1950 book *The Lonely Crowd* calls "an exceptional sensitivity to the actions and wishes of others." Riesman's depiction of middle-class life in the age of increased service jobs, bureaucracies, salaried executives, and media moguls suggests that the cocktail party is a microcosm of a larger human drama about self-exploration verging on black comedy.

In 1960, Riesman went on to cowrite a four-year sociological study of cocktail parties for the National Institute of Mental Health of the U.S. Public Health Service. Between January 1955 and December 1959, six anonymous confederates posed as partygoers to investigate eighty cocktail parties that took place primarily in New York and

Boston. In their article entitled "The Vanishing Host," the participants (acknowledging the problem of total recall after so many festive nights) concluded that such diversions as charades, bridge, and "projective" painting sessions were not enough to deflect a trend by which party hosts progressively lost territorial control. Guests had a tendency to veer off into private and same-sex conversation cliques; the unmarried scanned potential dates. Hosts, in turn, lost interest in trying to keep everyone excited and just made sure everyone was adequately replenished.

Host control over the cocktail party is always a problem and challenge. *Emily Post's Etiquette* claims: "Either the host or the hostess should stay within sight of the door to greet arriving guests, but they should try to avoid being out of the room where the party is held at the same time. They should not go to the door to greet their guests with drinks in their hands."

Cole Porter made sure his guests received no more than two cocktails before dinner. Regardless of who arrived late, he would start dinner at a precise time to avoid excessive drinking. This obsession with party symmetry and decorum intensified on one occasion when a friend invited some naïve young editor who committed the faux pas of asking for a cocktail after the meal began. A petulant Porter assented, but hovered over the man until the last drop was gone.

The cocktail party, like the cocktail lounge, has a magic-lantern show of lighting, decor, architectural angles, and sound. In 1959, Dr. William R. MacLean, an electrical engineering professor from the Polytechnic Institute of

Brooklyn, released *On the Acoustics of Cocktail Parties.* MacLean's observations calculated each interaction between human and libation according to reverberation time, room dimensions, and signal-to-noise ratio. For instance, a fifteen-by-fourteen-foot living room could sufficiently accommodate sixteen people, provided the ceilings were high enough. But if a seventeenth guest were to enter, the outcome would be what a *Newsweek* journalist reporting on the study called "a 100-proof brawl."

MacLean maintained the following after conducting much of his research at friends' get-togethers: "The significant thing is that the party doesn't get progressively louder. It suddenly goes from quiet to loud when there is one guest too many, or as they say in nuclear physics, when it 'goes critical.'"

Mr. Boston's Official Bartender's and Party Guide imparts wisdom when warning that "alcohol is a liquid good for preserving almost everything except secrets." Cocktail parties, though seemingly congenial affairs, can also be excuses for character intimidation. This is especially true at work-related get-togethers that encourage garrulity, though many wait for the slightest verbal or physical indiscretion that could damage someone's reputation or job security.

To enhance this party paranoia, a San Francisco private eye named Hal Lipset had impressed a U.S. Senate subcommittee in 1965 with a surveillance Martini. Inside the olive was a small transmitter and microphone that could enable party hosts to wander from guest to guest, or simply leave their drink in a strategic place, to pick up any valuable morsels of conversation. The only catch was that

Sean Connery. Though known for promoting the vodka Martini in his numerous James Bond films, Sean Connery also gave glamour to scotch whiskey. Connery's Bond emerged as one of the most memorable sixties cocktail personalities. He may have been a Brit in His Majesty's Secret Service, but he adopted the poses, values, and culinary tastes of a cocksure American imperialist transfixed (and somewhat psychologically castrated) by a bevy of technological toys. (Permission courtesy of Jim Beam Brands Co., Deerfield, Ill.)

liquid in the glass would cause a short, so the spy would always have to appear as if between drinks.

A common cocktail party demon is the *octopus comment* that lingers on the psyche like a multiple-armed beast. It could be a double message or sundry stab at sarcasm shrouded in a halfhearted compliment. John Cheever's short story "The Cure" presents a fine example: The protagonist is at a cocktail party considering infidelity while his wife and children are away. A female acquaintance, sensing he is vulnerable, comes up to him and flippantly suggests he will hang himself. From then on, he is haunted by the image of a dangling noose everywhere he goes.

Memorably maladroit moments are another problem. Gerald Clarke relates a perfect example in his biography of Truman Capote: When Truman was still a young up-and-coming writer in New York literary circles, he attended a cocktail party given by socialite Carmen Snow. He was handed a glass of milk because Snow assumed the diminutive and cherubic author was a youngster. When someone explained who he was and described his nightmarish stories, she immediately served him the appropriate Martini.

Despite its drawbacks, the cocktail hour is still an enchanting experiment in time. It can transform a life, launch a career, or ignite a romance in a matter of minutes. It can even be a substitute for romance. As Nic Van Oudtshoorn claims in *The Hangover Handbook*: "The energy expended by humans in a single act of lovemaking is the same as that needed to stand at cocktail parties and make small talk for about eight hours."

11

Rat Pack Cabala

You didn't go to sleep, you passed out. From now on you get cocktails *or* wine, not cocktails *and* wine!

—John Cassavetes, *Rosemary's Baby*

The 1960s—a kaleidoscope of hypnosis, madness, and damnation—owes much of its charm to the election of America's first Roman Catholic president. The American presidency, once a Protestant stronghold, became in John Fitzgerald Kennedy's hands an arena of sin, momentary redemption, flashy pageantry, antipapist conspiracy theories, and dashy cocktail parties at both the White House and Hyannisport. JFK was, after all, the son of an ex-whiskey smuggler and movie producer, who barely squeaked past with the tightest electoral margin in American history, thanks in no small part to the vote-getting efforts of his whiskey-loving chums—the ultracool, ultraswinging Rat Pack.

Columnist Earl Wilson, who spent a great amount of time chronicling Sinatra's career, described JFK as "the sexiest, swingingest President of the century." It was natural then that Sinatra, the swingingest singer, would help to mold the presidential image once Rat Packer Peter Lawford forged a lifeline by marrying JFK's sister Patricia. Collaborating with Lawford, Sinatra got JFK the best hi-fi and stereo system, initiated him into the classiest of casino fraternities, and threw him an inaugural party so lush and so "wet" that Eleanor Roosevelt, on hand for the festivities, made bluenose comments on its inordinate number of tipplers.

The Rat Pack era is renowned not only for bolstering Kennedy's election but for binding American politics to the entertainment industry. These were the new gentlemen of leisure, whose cavalier antics had sparked existential hunger in a world-weary middle class finally convinced that the "good life" had nothing to do with an afterlife. All the Depression babies who had won the Big War could get at least some kind of door prize with a trip to Vegas, a stab at the slot machine, and Highballs to keep them fueled.

The Rat Pack was indeed a Hollywood product, spawned by the supreme film noir couple Humphrey Bogart and Lauren Bacall. Bacall, who became Mrs. Bogart, supposedly coined the term *Rat Pack* during the late fifties when it was still a small cabal of swingers hanging out in Los Angeles's Holmby Hills.

The Rat Pack was, in Earl Wilson's words, "a do-nothing organization devoted to nonconformity and whiskey-drinking." It was an Algonquin Round Table for self-styled cads and cad-ettes that included Sinatra, Irving "Swifty" Lazar, Sid Luft, Judy Garland, Joey Bishop, Sammy Davis Jr., Shirley MacLaine, and others who

Sinatra and Bacall. With Bogie gone, Frank Sinatra and Lauren Bacall became the Rat Pack's king and queen. The moody widow and the punchy crooner came to embody a new kind of cool: swanky clothes, a leisurely travel itinerary, and a zest for nightlife that inspired John and Jackie Kennedy's White House for swingers. (Michael Ochs Archives, Venice, Calif.)

basked in sensational press and took frequent party cruises on Bogart's sixty-five-foot yacht, the *Santana* (named after the vessel Bogie commandeered in *Key Largo*).

After Bogart died of cancer in January 1957, Sinatra became the premier Rat Packer, while Bacall retained her place as "den mother." By now, Sinatra was already entering his career's "ring-a-ding-ding" phase, with a Best Supporting Actor Oscar under his belt and a crooner career shift from Axel Stordahl's romantically lush arrangements to Nelson Riddle's swing. Sinatra intoned, "It's witchcraft!" on his 1958 hit, not knowing how much those words to this now immortal Cy Coleman song portended the occult quirks about to unfold.

In 1960, while still garnering Kennedy votes, the Rat Pack was already filming *Ocean's 11*. Released a year before Nicholas Ray's *King of Kings, Ocean's 11* provided what could be interpreted as an ingenious satire on Christ's apostles (minus one), made just as Vatican II was making earth-shattering changes. Directed by Lewis Milestone and shot on location on the resplendent boulevards of Vegas, the plot involves eleven former paratroopers of the Eighty-second Airborne who attempt to storm the money-lending temples of Vegas's Sahara, Desert Inn, Sands, Flamingo, and Riviera.

Second to its hints of sacrilege were the film's assaults on the holy canons of high art. Two years previous, French avant-gardist Yves Klein (notorious for using women doused in blue dye as his human paintbrushes) had invited ogling guests to Paris's Iris Clert Gallery for cocktails and a room full of blank canvases. Feeling bewildered, miffed, and ripped off, the guests did not attain their artistic revelation until they got home and, thanks to a special something in their libations, pissed *bleu*.

But the brashly Yankee Rat Packers had no time for such diuretic dalliance. They instead advocated a more populist cocktail color theory by promoting the amber waves of distilled grain rolling in a glass of scotch whiskey. Instead of Klein's blank room, Frank and his sharkskin-suited pallies filled their spaces with Vegas's neon signs, plush carpets, tribal African sculpture, Christmas trees, mechanical Santas, pseudo-abstract wall paintings, and one-armed bandits—all coordinated with the predominant ocher, à la *Jacques* Daniel's.

Ocean's 11 may also have been a sly allusion to an alleged Las Vegas "Black Book," which had legally barred eleven of the FBI's most wanted underworld figures from all casinos. Whatever, the film's preoccupation with numbers invites a treasure trove of numerological references possibly drawn from the Cabala.

Much of the story revolves around a "Law of Fives" (that is explained in such occult books as *Illuminatus!* by Robert Shea and Robert Anton Wilson). Accordingly, the number five plays an important role in mystical thinking. For some it could be the holiest of numbers, for others the most unlucky. The pentagram, for instance, is considered the supreme symbol of occult power, the five-sided star that evokes demons. In the Cabala, *five* signifies a primitive fear of the unknown and the superstitions from which most religions originate.

Surrounding the *Ocean's 11* rituals of leisure and worldly gain are objects and themes amounting either to five or divisibles and multiples of five: the decision to rob five casinos; the ten letters in Danny Ocean's name; subjecting Las Vegas to fifteen minutes of darkness while they carry out their heist; the 8+2 in Ocean's "82nd" Airborne, and, of course, Ocean's diminution to ten members when a key operative dies from a heart attack.

The Rat Pack starts to look more like the membership to some Masonic lodge when Ocean's 10 pay their respects to the dead crony and guard the loot they had stashed away safely with the corpse. The eye-in-the-triangle symbol that looms inside the Vegas chapel is not only the emblem on every dollar bill but also the "eye of Horus" that Masons are known to invoke during their otherworldly meetings. (Another variation appears in the triangular Martini glass, with the olive's pimento-pupil gazing at its beholder.) The Rat Pack incurs the cosmic joke's brunt, however, cringing helplessly as they hear the crematorium's oven.

Ocean's 11 also introduced the public to the Rat Pack lexicon. Death was "the big casino," God was "the big G," and Packers allegedly addressed Sinatra as "the pope." The latter became an ironic title when Sinatra had his publicist arrange an in-depth interview for the February 1963 issue of *Playboy*. When asked if he believed in God, Sinatra gave what some could interpret as an antipapist reply: "I'm for *anything* that gets you through the night, be it prayer, tranquilizers, or a bottle of Jack Daniel's. But to me religion is a

Rat Pack Pack Rat? In 1966, India's ambassador B. N. Chakravarty claimed: "The Americans are a funny lot. They drink whiskey to keep them warm; then they put some ice in it to make it cool. They put sugar in it to make it sweet, and then they put a slice of lemon in it to make it sour. Then they say 'Here's to you' and drink it themselves." Here, Sammy Davis Jr. demonstrates that even solitary drinking requires agile diplomacy. (Michael Ochs Archives, Venice, Calif.)

deeply personal thing in which man and God go it alone to-gether, without the witch doctor in the middle."

Not even Sinatra's controversial religious sentiments could upstage JFK being gunned down in Dealey Plaza on November 22, 1963. With the king destroyed and only the followers to carry the crown, the "New Frontier" began to go awry. Logic and proportion subsided as more and more Americans started talking backwards with lurid tales of conspiracies and secret numerical clues emblazoned on U.S. currency, even drawing parallels to Lincoln's murder. With this social shift came a more dolorous cocktail existential-ism, a quieter counterculture bewitching the very people a future vice-president would label "the silent majority."

Meanwhile, a barload of cocktail companions started aiding many moviegoers during these darker years. Holly-wood, always the mainstream's social barometer, released several films that accompanied their drinking scenes with *large* thoughts about middle-class morality and the kind of delirium tremens eternity might have in store.

Jim Backus as the bibulous Mr. Fitzgerald in *It's a Mad, Mad, Mad, Mad World* (1963) gives an object lesson in the foibles of excessive drinking. While flying his charter plane on a mad chase for hidden loot, he presses the button marked "Booze" in his hideaway bar to whip up more than one Old-Fashioned. Though claiming "it's the only way to fly," he ends up an inebriated Icarus, passed out after consuming a whole case of bourbon and leaving the flying to Mickey Rooney and Buddy Hackett. One scene in the social satire *Good Neighbor Sam* (1964) has Jack Lemmon doing spastic dance steps with next door neighbor Romy Schneider while under the Martini influence, both pretending to be husband and wife so that Schneider can meet the demands of her grandfather's will and collect an inheritance. *Who's Afraid of Virginia Woolf?* came out two years later, with Elizabeth Taylor as Martha the gin harpy, who chugs it on the rocks endlessly and literally bays at the full moon. The equally stewed Richard Burton (the troubled husband both on and off camera) gets his revenge by reminding her about the child they could never have and the American dream they could never attain.

Among the most spiritually apocalyptic of sixties movies was *The Swimmer* (1968). Based on John Cheever's short story, it starred Burt Lancaster as a beleaguered upper-class drone who decides to swim from work to his Connecticut home via a route of backyard pools. On his affluent odyssey, he encounters the dangerous acquaintances who own these pools, each attempting to feed his head with cocktails. Between intermittent sips of clarified gin, he tries to purify his soul with chlorinated water. The first scene, as Lancaster surfaces after a graceful dive, is dominated by a "diluted Martini" that one of his reluctant hosts places in the foreground. Each new pool holds more cocktail offers, but the overripe baptismal metaphor is soon tainted when it becomes obvious that Lancaster has no real home or family waiting for him. *Variety* astutely called the film "the story of a moral hangover."

That same year, Paramount released what is arguably the most telling movie about what many anticipated as the end-of-the-sixties millennia, the film version of Ira Levin's novel *Rosemary's Baby.* Before getting caught up in the ungodly murder of his wife, Sharon Tate, and its resulting Manson saga, director Roman Polanski put into cinematic form a psychedelic tapestry of subliminal seductions and innuendo that links Kennedy's presidency, the Rat Pack, sixties occultism, cocktail parties, and what some celebrity clerics at the time went so far as to call the "death of God theology."

Mixing the occult and cocktails with the fashionable argot of LSD culture, Polanski paints a cross-section of interlocking destinies that satisfies author Levin's heady descriptions. Rosemary Woodhouse (Mia Farrow) and her husband, Guy (John Cassavetes), find an apartment in New York City's "The Bramford" (The Dakota). The Woodhouses soon make friends with two key players in a witch coven who occupy the next-door apartment. The devil worshippers make a deal with Guy to boost his flagging acting career provided he lends them his wife to bear Satan's only begotten son.

As in the novel, the unaware Rosemary gets prepared for the rite with a sedative-laced chocolate mousse, but the book elaborates on her mistake of combining a near lethal combination of two or three glasses of wine, two Gibsons, and a crème de menthe. From there, the story drifts into Rosemary's dream.

Polanski's dream sequence opens with Rosemary on a yacht, enjoying drinks at an on-deck cocktail soiree that has an entourage of beautiful women surrounding JFK. Levin's novel identifies Peter Lawford's wife, Pat (that connubial link between the White House and the Vegas Sands), among the group, along with Winston Churchill's daughter Pamela.

Kennedy explains to a bewildered Rosemary the party's "Catholics only" policy before Jackie Kennedy approaches Rosemary at the sacrificial bed to assure her that everything will be fine. The dream closes with Pope Paul, who interrupts his visit to Yankee Stadium to make his witch-doctor house call, brandishing a talismanic ring for Rosemary to kiss. (An early scene in Levin's novel has Rosemary reading *Manchild in the Promised Land*. In the film, Polanski might have established a cause and effect for Rosemary's Rat Pack incubi by having her read Sammy Davis Jr.'s autobiography, *Yes I Can*.)

Ira Levin had specified in *Rosemary's Baby* that the demon child would be born in the summer of 1966. In real life, Anton LaVey (who would appear in Polanski's film as the Satan cameo) had hailed 1966 as the Year One, celebrating his newly formed Church of Satan that spring with a cocktail party at his San Francisco mansion during *Walpurgisnacht*. That same summer, *Time* magazine ran a cover story asking "Is God Dead?" and Frank Sinatra married Mia Farrow. These two latter events are at best tenuously related, but the parallel between reports about the death of God and the waning of the Rat Pack is whimsically foreboding.

With Kennedy's Camelot fading into history and the bad boys of *Ocean's 11* slouching toward squaredom, Sinatra would soon grow weary of the sixties limelight, a fatigue prompted no doubt by the generational discord between himself and his new wife. The cocktail grandeur was over. It was time to bow out with grace, if only temporarily. In the 1957 film *The Joker Is Wild*, Sinatra referred to marriage as "two fast years and a cocktail shaker." Divorcing Farrow in 1968, he was true to his word. That was not the case, however, three years later when he announced he would retire from show business. Performing his farewell concert in June 1971 at the Los Angeles Music Center, Sinatra closed by acknowledging the debt he owed to saloon songs, ending with "Angel Eyes," and leaving the stage in a literal puff of smoke from his cigarette. He almost had the world believing the end was near.

The Beauty at *Butterfield 8*. Elizabeth Taylor's screen career provides a reference point for the many sides of America's drinking character. In *The Big Hangover,* she played an ingenue trying to nurse boyfriend Van Johnson back to sobriety; in *Who's Afraid of Virginia Woolf?,* she was Martha the gin harpy haranguing her husband and coddling memories of a nonexistent child. But it was in *Butterfield 8* that Liz captured the erotic wonders and existential horrors of being America's combination sweetheart, sex symbol, and shrew. Here, she played a call-girl trying to make good by romancing a browbeating Laurence Harvey. In one key scene, she dons a pearl necklace and black velvet gloves to sip Martinis at a nightclub with him. But when an angry Liz cannot have her way, she exposes the situation's false elegance by grinding her stiletto heel into Mr. Harvey's foot. While in Rome on the set of the 1973 film *The Driver's Seat* (in which she plays a dazed tourist in search of her ideal murderer), Liz reportedly gorged herself on a drink she called a "Debauched Mary," consisting, in her words, of "five parts vodka and one part blood." (©1960 Turner Entertainment Co. All Rights Reserved.)

12

Being Had
(The Sociology of "Girl Drinks")

I thought he said it was a lady's drink; I *think* he meant a lady horse.

—Shirley MacLaine, *Ocean's 11*

In November 1969—months after the Manson murders and one month before scores of hippies at Altamont genuflected to Satan-impersonator Mick Jagger and his Hell's Angels—San Francisco unveiled a landmark called "Henry Africa," the first official fern bar. At last, a sign that the Age of Aquarius had truly budded, and from its pseudomystic stage, would blossom into a leisure industry. In no time head shops became boutiques— a positive sign that transcendental meditation would one day succumb to contemplation of the Fuzzy Navel.

Baby boomers weaned on white bread, endless candy, and constant sensation grew accustomed to spectacle and media-created "happenings." In search of new short-lived fads, they, like the gullible prom queen, were ready to be had. This was especially true by the midseventies, when many reports about CIA-linked LSD experiments only reinforced the notion that there was a fine line between social manipulation and recreational culture.

The flurry of media immersion theories was so intense that many grew uncertain, and some rarely cared, whether the social critics exposing the manipulation around us were any less manipulative. For instance, Wilson Bryan Key, in his book *Subliminal Seduction*, claims that one particular Bacardi rum ad from the seventies contains a "symbolic menagerie" of skulls, masks, bats, and death icons in an attempt to imply "that one might richly enjoy dying if well fortified with Bacardi rum or, quite possibly, Bacardi will serve to protect the drinker from a fear of death." He also attempts to show how a Gilbey's London Dry Gin ad appearing on the back cover of *Time* in July 1971 had the word "sex" cleverly inscribed on the ice cubes inside a Tom Collins. He even points out the ghostly forms of a vagina and clitoris reflected between the Collins glass and the Gilbey's bottle. Key's thesis is that Gilbey's attempted to sell its liquor "through a subliminal appeal to latent voyeuristic or exhibitionistic tendencies within the unconscious minds of *Time* readers."

Whether or not a liquor ad's ice cubes couched hieroglyphics of sex and death, such ideas were too elaborate and alluring not to be enjoyed. Exposés of the media's chicanery made potential dupes paradoxically less innocent yet voraciously gullible. Like lambs to the slaughter, somewhat aware of where they were heading, consumers were ready to lie back, close their eyes, and relinquish all sales resistance. No wonder, then, that with alcohol consumption, something as staid as the dry Martini creed took a backseat to a renewed demand for sensation drinks.

Writing for *Esquire* in 1973, James Villas claimed that the Martini "stands for everything from phony bourgeois values and social snobbery to jaded alcoholism and latent masochism." In the Martini's stead came "girl drinks"— those elaborate concoctions that flout all pretense at "good taste" and embrace prolonged adolescence. Hard-boiled drinkers might hate them, but girl drinks are among cocktail culture's greatest assets. Their multicolored hues, sugary excesses, and twee names give hope that the art of drink mixing continues to evolve and that cocktails are more than just spartan exercises.

Food historian Barbara Kafka summarizes the seventies girl-drink rebirth best: "There was a huge demographic shift. Suddenly we had the yuppie bulge, post-war kids who consumed of that hideous sweet wine that had liquor but did not taste like liquor. The fern bars were a symptom of people who just don't like the taste of booze."

Sure, the dry Martini can be wonderful and cleansing, but its monastic simplicity gets too dull without at least an occasional saccharine safari into gum sugar, molasses, maraschino cherries, grenadine, orgeat syrup, fruit juice, heavy cream, and various other confections.

In the fern bar's wake, the seventies also produced "disco cocktails," matching aesthetics for Tiffany glasses, cotillion balls, track lighting, and Maxfield Parrish wall posters. This hedonistic era also harbored growing anti-alcohol sentiments. Betty Ford's infamous bouts with dipsomania spawned a clinic in her name. Rosalynn Carter proclaimed a moratorium on serving hard liquor at White House functions. Jimmy Carter lampooned excessive government perks with his infamous "three-Martini lunch" speech (though he was essentially griping about the "$50 Martini lunch").

There was also a dearth of appropriate role models. Cocktail culture was now getting backed into a ghetto of middle-aged obsolescence that was as confining as the studio prop bar setup for Dean Martin on his NBC television show. Such cocktail doyens as Martin were put into leisure suits for spots on television movies-of-the-week or all-star disaster "epics." As Nora Charles in the thirties *Thin Man* movies, Myrna Loy drank her Martinis with upper-crust aplomb. But when she appeared in *Airport 1975,* she was a bedraggled Hollywood has-been, reduced to chugging boilermakers to get her mind off a perilous flight.

Earlier, in 1972, the *Reader's Digest,* which never published any advertisement connected with liquor, ran a public service message from Seagram's on the perils of drinking and driving. The ad displayed someone writing "I can drive when I drink" repeatedly, the sentence getting less legible with each sip they take.

Perhaps this atmosphere of caution and disillusion propelled drinkers to neutralize alcohol with its sugary adversary. Heywood Gould's 1984 novel *Cocktail* provides a revealing account of the "fancy cocktail" popularity that started in the late 1960s. His lead character, Brian Flanagan, is a liberal arts veteran with a useless college degree, thwarted ambitions to be a writer, and a general tendency to float from one hostile sexual relationship to the next. In his thirties with nothing better to do, he goes on a picaresque bartender adventure, getting his first job at a popular Upper East Side singles club: "The saloon culture was expanding to include people who had very little experience with alcohol, and would have been much happier in an ice cream parlor. The liquor companies responded to this new market by creating recipes for its childish palate, improbable, dyspeptic combinations of liquors, fruit juices, and heavy cream. 'Coronary cocktails' and 'nickname drinks' . . . "

The seventies offered a renaissance, but girl drinks have a prior history. The term *girl drink* does not *necessarily* imply a drink for "sissies." Its original designation describes drinks purposely tailored for naïve female dates who would be more prone to say *yes* after such taste temptations got them unwittingly high. They have also been called "prom cocktails," probably because, like debutantes, girl drinks often come with fixtures resembling frilly gowns, parasols, and ringlets.

The term *girl drink* could, in many respects, be considered redundant. By the time Victorian-style saloons popped up in nineteenth-century America, you did not usually find any man's hand attached to a cocktail. William Grimes, in *Straight Up or On the Rocks,* summarizes the prejudices of the time by flatly stating: "Cocktails were for sissies. The drinks were whiskey, drunk straight, and beer."

Among the most notorious of girl drinks is the Brandy Alexander. This concoction of brandy, crème de cacao, and regular sweet cream was reportedly a favorite among Prohibition-era teenagers who wanted to ape their parents

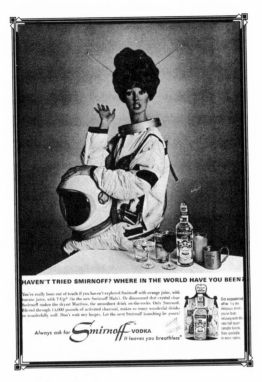

HAVEN'T TRIED SMIRNOFF? WHERE IN THE WORLD HAVE YOU BEEN?

You've really been out of touch if you haven't explored Smirnoff with orange juice, with tomato juice, with 7-Up® (in the new Smirnoff Mule). Or discovered that crystal clear Smirnoff makes the dryest Martinis, the smoothest drink on-the-rocks. Only Smirnoff, filtered through 14,000 pounds of activated charcoal, makes so many wonderful drinks so wonderfully well. Don't wait any longer. Let the next Smirnoff launching be yours!

Always ask for *Smirnoff* VODKA
It leaves you breathless®

Get acquainted offer. Try the delicious drinks you've been missing with this new half-quart sampler bottle. Now available in most stores.

Smirnoff Space Girl. Cocktails and cosmic ecstasy. An American astronette advertises Russian vodka to remind the world that both *astro-* and *cosmo-* nauts would have rather shared drinks than fight the Cold War. Cocktails are somehow embedded into the righteous and sometimes thwarted dreams of the Space Age. Contemporary space travelers are visionaries who may often need a cocktail's simulated weightlessness to cope with a mundane anticlimax awaiting them after splashdown. Example: Jack Nicholson's enigmatic role as the tippling ex-astronaut in the film *Terms of Endearment*. (Heublein, Inc.)

without relinquishing their passion for chocolate bars. As drink critic Maurice Zolotow wrote in a 1966 issue of *Playboy*: "After three or four alexanders, the girl would experience a strange and overpoweringly erotic sensation all through her body, and if the time and the place were right, she became not only willing but ardent. More girls probably became pregnant as a result of guzzling brandy alexanders than from any other single cause during the 1920s."

Blake Edwards's film *Days of Wine and Roses* made this Brandy Alexander principle pivotal to the story. In the original J. P. Miller teleplay, the two principal characters are already mired in alcohol abuse when they meet and fall in love. But the film makes the woman (Lee Remick) a teetotaler and chocolate connoisseur lured by her seasoned beau (Jack Lemmon) into having her first Alexander, a prelude to a life and marriage doomed literally for the rocks.

Many girl drinks have become legendary. The Singapore Sling was a favorite of such figures as Somerset Maugham, Joseph Conrad, and Douglas Fairbanks. Invented at Singapore's Raffles Hotel, its standard ingredients called for a shot of gin, cherry brandy, a teaspoon of sugar, juice of one-half lemon, and a dash of bitters, all poured over ice in a Collins glass, topped with soda, and garnished with a cherry or a lemon or orange wedge.

The Pink Squirrel, reportedly conceived during the transatlantic deco days of the thirties, is what Heywood Gould in *Cocktail* describes as one of the "complicated cocktails." It combines the lactic maw of heavy cream, the effete abuses of white crème de cacao and crème de noyau, and the Shirley Temple stigma of grenadine syrup, shaken with ice and topped with a deadly sweet maraschino cherry.

Umbrella drinks were also emblematic of the post–World War II infatuation with the South Seas. Victor "Trader Vic" Bergeron would often promote gimmicky cocktails as part of a public-relations campaign for various cruise liners. At his Oakland restaurant in 1944, he combined seventeen-year-old rum from Jamaica, the juice from a fresh lime, a few dashes of Dutch orange curaçao syrup, some French orgeat, and rock candy syrup. He then leavened it with enough shaved ice to fill a glass. After a vigorous shake, and with a half lime shell and fresh mint as garnish, Bergeron presented the drink to two of his friends from Tahiti. One of them sipped it and proclaimed "Mai Tai—Roa Ae," which in Tahitian means "Out of this world—the best!" At that moment, according to Trader Vic history anyway, the Mai Tai was born. It was such a success that Bergeron went abroad to the Hawaiian Islands via the Matson Steamship Lines to promote the Mai Tai for the Royal Hawaiian, Surfsider, and Mauna hotels. He also brought it along as part of the regular bar regimen for the American President Lines in 1954.

One characteristic of a girl drink is its ability, above all other drinks, to tell fascinating stories. Its convoluted contours and multicolors can be as entertaining as watching a Vegas cakewalk. Thomas Hudson, the painter in Hemingway's *Islands in the Stream,* discovers the girl drink's narrative magic as he reflects on how the hues in his frozen Daiquiri rouse visions of oceans, ships, and a frappéed forest of seaweed caresses.

We should note that Hemingway, the macho literary icon, helped inspire a sugary, slushy drink often associated today with flowery tourist shirts. At the Floridita bar he made famous, Hemingway became an instant fan of a then sugarless mixture of lime and grapefruit juice, maraschino liquor, Bacardi White Label rum, and shaved ice. Bartender Constantino Ribailagua mixed them and later boasted of serving at least ten million frozen Daiquiris during his forty-year career. Because Hemingway was accustomed to always ordering doubles, the drink became known as "Papa Dobles."

At Harry's Bar in Venice, the mere mention of the Bellini—that piquant pink potation of one part peach juice and two parts champagne—made such aficionados as Hemingway and Noel Coward light up. In the late 1980s, it would make a comeback when Cipriani opened two New York restaurants and started marketing the Bellini as the optimal summer cocktail.

Post-sixties indulgers did come up with original concoctions. One sensation drink was the Harvey Wallbanger, reportedly invented at Pancho's Bar at California's Manhattan Beach. Other accounts trace it to the Galliano manufacturers who conjured up a fictitious surfer named Harvey to pitch a new drink to younger consumers. The Harvey legend paints him as a surfer who wiped out in a late-sixties surfing tournament and would anesthetize his wounded ego by drinking a sugary mix of Galliano and vodka. With too many of these in his system, Harvey would supposedly knock his head against walls and needed several bystanders to save him from a self-inflicted concussion.

Two popular songs reflected the timely tastes: Jimmy Buffett's "Margaritaville" and Rupert Holmes's "Escape (The Piña Colada Song)." Both hit *Billboard*'s Top 40, in 1977 and 1978 respectively. Even international politicians found it easier to say *yes* to diplomatic decrees with a Technicolor toddy in hand. In 1973, a Savoy Hotel bartender in London celebrated Britain's entry into the ECC by devising a Common Market cocktail: Belgium's Elixir d'Anu, Denmark's cherry brandy, France's dry vermouth, West Germany's Schlichte, Britain's sloe gin, The Netherlands's curaçao, Luxembourg's dry white wine, Ireland's coffee liqueur, and Italy's Caprano.

Perhaps the most controversial girl drink invasion was that of the Shooter. Though not officially considered a "girl drink," the Shooter's flamboyant mixtures and appeals to candied intoxication make it differ very little from an Angel's Tit. The simple act of chugging a shot of whiskey got refurbished in the late seventies and early eighties with such creations as the B-52, the Kamikaze, and the Cordless Screwdriver. Like most girl drinks, Shooters' alcohol content is deceptively camouflaged. They are often a mixture of liqueurs and fruit juices, served in odd-shaped goblets or test tubes frequently called "tooters," in baubles worn around the neck.

Sex-on-the-Beach, for instance, mixes black raspberry liqueur with melon liqueur, pineapple and/or cranberry juice, and vodka. The Parisian Blonde has equal parts light rum, Jamaican rum, and triple sec. A combination of Irish creme, coffee, and hazelnut liqueurs with vodka and amaretto creates an International Incident. By the early 1980s, with such concoctions as peach schnapps commercially available, the Fuzzy Navel's blend of orange juice and peach schnapps got served up in a standard Highball glass. The Girl Drink Generation had truly arrived.

The "mocktail" was the next logical step: a drink with cocktail trappings but no sting. Eventually, the cocktail's theatrics would grow so strong that the mere *appearance* of having a real one was all that mattered. Many mocktails are alcohol-free versions of established drinks, such as the Virgin Mary (Bloody Mary with just the blood), which ex-drinkers often enjoy as an easy substitute.

No discussion of mocktails or girl drinks can ignore the archetypal Shirley Temple. It is the most ersatz mocktail and arguably the first authentic one. In sketch comedy, Jack Benny would be the constant butt of jokes when he would take the role of the oddball out drinking with the boys, ordering Shirley Temples while the rest indulged in the hard stuff. This mixture of ginger ale and a dash of grenadine with a maraschino cherry became such a stereotype through the years that in 1984 the maraschino cherry industry decided to sponsor a contest to concoct the best name and recipe to replace "Shirley." Eleven judges converged in New York to award the $500 prize to a Wyoming, Minnesota, woman for providing the name; two women, one from Beaverdale, Pennsylvania, and the other from Alden, New York, shared an additional $500 for thinking up the recipe. The new drink was the Zinger, consisting of three parts orange to one part maraschino cherry juice, poured over ice and topped with both an orange slice *and* a cherry.

Girl drinks continue to represent a kind of psycho-sexual labyrinth for those brave and nobly neurotic enough to enter. For self-styled sophisticates, however, they pose a threat, a constant temptation to regress to the child in all of us, that simpering weakling who never outgrew mother's milk. Girl drinks, for this reason, have had vehement detractors. Back in the fifties, Bernard DeVoto (who in *The Hour* snarled at even the relatively puritanical gesture of placing an olive in a Martini) had the following sentiments: "An ice-cream soda can set a child's feet in the path that ends in grenadine, and when you see someone drinking drambuie, crème de menthe, Old Tom gin, or all three stirred together and topped off with a maraschino cherry, you must remember that he got that way from pineapple milk-shakes long ago. Pity him if you like but treat him as you would a carrier of typhoid. For if the Republic ever comes crashing down, the ruin will have been wrought by this lust for sweet drinks."

But for every such sour note, there are many sweet drinks to drown it out. Even the stolid Martini has had its share of mad mixologists and interior designers attempting to rearrange his genes and put him in skirts. From time to time, even in the dankest and dreariest of bars, where the hard-nosed and rock-faced drink only shots and blend into a stale gray cigarette haze, there will be that special, intrepid soul who dares add color to the place by ordering an umbrella drink and with a mischievous smile says, "Care to join me?"

13

The Frankenstein Martini
(Mangled, Not Shaken!)

In its rite, the Martini exercises a communal function. The host or paterfamilias who mixes the drinks acts as priest, and families or friends are united as devotees of the cult.

—Lowell Edmunds, *The Silver Bullet*

The following recipe combines mixing Martinis with saving souls: Pour your favorite gin (or vodka) with a few dashes of your favorite vermouth into a decanter over ice; shake a few times; then, with the chilled cocktail glass ready at your side, pour the entire contents into a blender and press the "ice crush" button for precisely four seconds. The result: a chainsaw-massacre Martini that is delicious, cold, wild, free, and bathed in a sea of cathartic violence.

For years, the cult of the cocktail has centered on an ecumenical rift between those advocating the consummately dry Martini and those seeking to play havoc with its genetic structure. Being the pampered pet of purists, the Martini has always flirted with at least an occasional violation. The strict Martini recipe provides a stable springboard from which mixologists have been able to indulge in a variety of deviations. FDR was among the first major figures to boldly add variant ingredients to his favorite drink. Lowell Edmunds, in his exemplary book *The Silver Bullet,* provides an exhaustive study of Martinis and points out that FDR "saw no reason not to add fruit juice to Martinis, or Pernod, or Anisette." Roosevelt's secretary Grace Tully revealed in her memoirs that the President inadvertently used aquavit instead of gin on one occasion.

The most spellbinding moments of Martini chemical warfare took place in the fifties, the same era that spawned horror movies about nuclear mutations and scientific excursions into creative disfigurement. One strong force was novelist Ian Fleming, who had his Cold Warrior James Bond sabotage the Martini's traditionally gin-blooded American gene pool with Russian vodka, "shaken, not stirred." The popularity of Bond's vodka Martini prompted a state of siege among those who considered even the addition of an olive excessive.

In the novel *Casino Royale,* Bond compounds the outrage by combining three parts Gordon's gin to one of vodka, with an herbal wine similar to vermouth called Kina Lillet, shaken with ice and a lemon-peel slice. He called it "the Vesper," named after his doomed girlfriend and double agent Vesper Lynd.

Oddly enough, some figures having an impact on how America enjoys its Martinis hail from England. In contrast to Fleming, author W. Somerset Maugham took a more delicate approach by insisting that Martinis should never be shaken lest it bruise the gin and upset the molecules that "lie sensuously on top of each other . . . " But as far back as 1930, Harry Craddock of London's Savoy Hotel wrote in the *Savoy Cocktail Book*: "Shake the shaker as hard as you can: don't just rock it: you are trying to wake it up, not send it to sleep."

Perhaps inspired by Fleming's transgression, British author Kingsley Amis invented a variation on the vodka Martini based on his novel *Lucky Jim*. The "Lucky Jim" consists of twelve to fifteen parts vodka to one part dry vermouth; only this time the essential added kicker is cucumber juice, along with a garnish of cucumber slices, all poured over ice.

American marketing, however, has been the most potent force in converting the Martini into a liquor promoter's petri dish. By the early fifties, the liquor-dealing firm of Otis & Lee sponsored a Martini recipe contest from which it salvaged 25 out of 240 suggestions on how to revamp the old formula. They included the addition of garlic, sauterne, Pernod, anchovy-stuffed olives, and the rinsing of a Martini glass in Cointreau. On another landmark occasion, one Johnny Solon, who was a mixologist at New York's old Waldorf, added orange juice with French and Italian vermouth to the original Martini formula and produced the "Bronx."

Replacing the Martini's olive with twists of lemon, anchovies, maraschino cherries, absinthe, crystallized violets, even Chanel No. 5 constitutes a minor infraction compared to the "Dillytini," an outlandish concoction that emerged from Washington, D.C., in 1959. This Martini was impaled by a two-inch pickled green bean.

Seagram's had launched several brilliant ad campaigns to reinvent the Martini. One seventies ad had a Japanese woman, in kimono, kneeling ceremonially as she stirred a Martini pitcher. It suggested a Martini miscegenation rite whereby a mere drop of sake could lend Seagram's gin an "Oriental" allure. In 1978, an ad depicted a suave couple in black evening garb drinking what was dubbed the "midnight Martini" because it sported a black instead of a green olive.

There are valid reasons for at least retaining the recipe for a Martini that is both dry and unadorned. Of all drinks, the Martini (with its pure, undiluted alcohol) is the most pristine high any drink can offer. It has a different impact on the body's blood sugar with a longer-lasting stimulus than most other concoctions sullied by juices, sugars, and creams. But the laws for dryness have themselves proven relative and transmutable.

If today's aficionados who favor a thirty-to-one ratio of gin to vermouth were to time-travel back to when Martinis first emerged as the supreme sign of urban elegance—the thirties—they might be surprised by what were then customary proportions of three to one. The rebellion against the "wet" Martini (some may call it vermouth-phobia) was more gradual. By the late 1950s, the House of Schenley took the dry fever to absurd extremes by recommending a Martini consisting only of a glass of chilled gin.

However, this time the gin was diluted from its customary 86 to 90 to a whimpering 80 proof.

As early as the forties, specialists had attempted to find out if Martinis have truly special properties. In 1941, a Dr. Giorgio Lolli studied the effects of various intoxicating beverages and found that Martinis had a similar blood alcohol curve to whiskey. Lolli returned to his investigation in 1964, when he helped conduct a series of electroencephalographic and electromyographic experiments on the alcohol reactions in several healthy men. The findings published in the *Quarterly Journal of Studies on Alcohol* suggested that wine was a stronger inebriant than Martinis.

It was Lolli who also suggested that a Martini's theatrics have transcendent effects. In his 1960 book *Social Drinking: How to Enjoy Drinking Without Being Hurt by It,* Lolli claims: "The graceful, long-stemmed and glittering glass; the cool and colorless transparency of the fluid stretching the curves of a pitted olive or the floating irregularities of a lemon peel convey the impression of a powerful stillness. . . ."

This "powerful stillness" is what most likely motivates strict Martini constructionists. Bernard DeVoto's highly opinionated cocktail assessment in his book *The Hour* described the Manhattan's substitution of whiskey for gin as "an offense against piety" since vermouth has no business commingling with the brown fluid.

The pursuit of dryness had led to predictable parody. At precisely twelve noon on August 16, 1963, a bartender at Boston's Nick's Restaurant declared that he had "succeeded in isolating the vermouth molecule." According to a Lowell, Massachusetts, citizen named Paul A. Pollock, a bottle of vermouth was present during an atomic test in White Sands, New Mexico. This allowed Pollock to promote the "fissionable Martini" made possible just by holding one's glass of gin out a window. M. Bertram Stanleigh, who was affiliated with the American Standards Association, put out his *Safety Code and Requirements for Dry Martinis* in 1966. Replete with graphs, tables, and footnotes, it was a satirical look at the association's sometimes doctrinaire literary style that nevertheless got reprinted in the early seventies when the association became the American National Standards Institute.

In 1975, Donald Gonzalez, an ex-Washington correspondent and then vice-president for Public Affairs of Colonial Williamsburg, sardonically surveyed the "debased" Martini by declaring: "Our day's-end marriage of good gin and vermouth is headed for the rocks! We are at the 11th hour—or even later—of a six o'clock disaster!"

But strict orthodoxy is meaningless without an attendant heresy to give it meaning. This makes variations on the Mangled Martini one of cocktail culture's most vital components. It was indeed vodka that inspired the Frankenstein Martini treatment, prompted largely by liquor marketeers who, like Disney's imagineers, have usually been successful at stimulating commerce with fun stratagems.

The first major alteration took place around the time that the "Smirnoff Leaves You Breathless" marketing

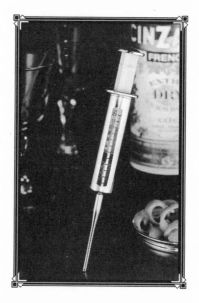

The Martini Spike. A squirt of vermouth or artificial insemination? Playing on the Martini purist's fears that vermouth is more a violation than a necessary ingredient, marketeers had produced such specialized clinical instruments as Gorham's "Martini Spike," with its calibrated syringe to let out just the right amount. There was also the "Vermouth Atomizer," which emitted discreet gusts that hovered over the glass with no direct contact. Hammacher Schlemmer brought us the "Vermouth Dropper." Lyman Metal Products had the Martini scale that came with a vessel for gin on one end and a thimble for vermouth at the other, to maintain a finicky proportion of 25:1. There were even vermouth-soaked Martini stones. To keep the drink as sterile as possible, Robert Stack's character Kyle Hadley, in the Douglas Sirk film *Written on the Wind,* offered the best solution. After finding out he is sperm-deficient, he fills Rock Hudson and Lauren Bacall in on his drink-mixing tip: "The secret is not to pour the vermouth, just to pretend you're pouring it." (Photograph by courtesy and permission of Gorham/Lenox Brands)

campaign flourished after World War II. Then there was the term *vodkatini* that circulated in the fifties. By 1967, thanks partly to the proliferation of Bond 007 movies, vodka surpassed gin as America's favorite distillate and then outranked whiskey nine years later.

With a revived interest in such retro icons as the "postmodern cocktail," the 1990s witnessed a renaissance that endowed mixology with the freedom Andy Warhol once gave to art: A Martini is anything you can get away with. In the fall of 1992, distiller representatives Schieffelin & Somerset hired Kirshenbaum & Bond to launch a grass-roots plan, hiring cocktail shills to hang out at swanky nightclubs and restaurants and pitch what Hennessy called its "*new* twist on a classic"—a Martini replacing gin and vodka mixtures with cognac and fresh lemon juice.

By September 1993, these walking infomercials multiplied, waiting until the peak hours on weekends to visit such places as the Royalton or Cafe Tabac and improvise situations where they would elaborate the cocktail's recipe to the bewildered bartender, within everyone's earshot, of course.

This somewhat successful drive to convince drinkers between ages twenty-five and forty-four that cognac could be a before- as well as an after-dinner drink is reminiscent of such previous ploys as the attractive woman who was reportedly dolled up in furs and hired to disembark from a limousine, walk into various New York clubs, approach the bartender, and do a petulant 180-degree turn back to the chauffeur upon hearing that the establishment did not serve J&B Scotch.

So, transmogrified Martinis are no longer a shock. They are, quite the contrary, key selling points for restaurants and clubs seeking to make ritual drinking as exciting and vital to daily commerce as it was in the days of postwar suburbia and gray-flannel suits. Such places as New York's Four Seasons Hotel have offered such items as a "Martini Only" menu, which includes the Candy Cane Martini, the Bellini Martini, and the Cosmopolitan Vodka Martini (cranberry-flavored vodka with a dash of Cointreau and cranberries replacing olives).

Dale DeGroff, the head bartender at New York's Rainbow Room, sees room for all kinds of Martini variations. When customers ask him for a dry Martini, he serves them a gin to vermouth ratio of thirty to one. When asked about the dry Martini orthodoxy, he avers: "The Martini is a fascinating drink because it has all the herbals in gin, mixed with all the herbals in vermouth. And a Martini *must* have vermouth. This business about just waving the bottle in front of the drink is nonsense."

In Seattle, a contingent of hotels and restaurants honors its favorite bartenders by hosting an annual "Martini Classic Challenge," a mix-off to determine the year's best drink. Even in Europe—always looking to the States for the proper cocktail fashions—a Gilbey's Gin ad featured an olive facing a Martini glass and challenging, "Go ahead, make my day." Another Gilbey's ad depicted a lemon parachuting toward a tall glass offering a cushion of gin.

Around the same time, Morton's of Chicago, a nationwide chain of steakhouses, unveiled a forty-Martini menu, alternating from gin to vodka and sundry compounds that lend new meaning to the phrase "Better living through chemistry." The drinks are grouped into three types: The Classics, The Contemporaries, and The *New* Traditionals. Among the creatures from their "Martini Club" are The Martinez (Bombay Gin, dry vermouth, bitters, maraschino liqueur, and a lemon slice); The Bootlegger Martini (Bombay Gin, Southern Comfort, and a lemon twist); The Cajun Martini (Absolut Peppar Vodka, dry vermouth, and a jalapeño pepper); The Kurant Affair (Absolut Kurant Vodka with raspberries); and The Dark Crystal (Stoli's Crystall Vodka, a splash of Remy Martin VSOP, and a lemon twist).

Perhaps the best way to understand and appreciate the Martini's psychic allure is by comparing it to a crystal ball. It looks clear on the surface until it clouds up with the lustrous and lurid thought projections of its drinker. It is a looking glass, a barometer for both personality and public image. The Martini could send the otherwise mild-mannered actor Montgomery Clift into adverse personality changes. It was also the talisman of choice for surrealist director Luis Buñuel, who preferred to drink them in the dark.

In the seventies, poet Anthony Hecht's "The Ghost in the Martini" used the drink as a supernatural truth serum. The poem narrates the lonely thoughts of a man eying a pretty young woman whose contours he sees reflected in his drink. As he contemplates when to make his amorous advance, he stares deeper, watching as the Martini goes "seeping down to the dark old id." But the more he looks, the more the devilish juniper juice starts talking back to him. Just a few more sips, and he soon sees himself as just one more poseur in a sea of frozen poses.

Shirley MacLaine, who went from being the Rat Pack's honorary female to achieving fame as a New Age crystal enthusiast, may have indirectly determined the course of gin and vodka advertising in the nineties as distillers began stressing the elemental purity of gin and vodka. Bombay's Sapphire Gin and Stolichnaya's Cristall Vodka have transformed the Martini once again, this time from a reconstituted monster to a transcendent angel.

Through the efforts of Stolichnaya, the great world events inspired salient packaging. Vodka would be seen as a tasteless, colorless, odorless substance whose mere possession entailed a paramount rapture. Stolichnaya's Cristall became a "superpremium" vodka since its ingredients are filtered not through gangly, earthy charcoal, but through the finer stuff of quartz.

One proposed Stolichnaya ad campaign depicted the sacred quartz crystals being lorded over by "ancient Chinese priests." Another proposed the more architectonic image of guards surrounding a Cristall vodka monument. After various focus-group evaluations, the ad campaign devised a mock-up of a Soviet Constructivist design which, though outwardly reminding us of Stalinism, ultimately invalidates the biblical paranoia about an Antichrist emerging from the East. The post–Cold War new world order distilled the anticipated war between Gog and Magog into a pan-democractic cocktail soiree in which Stolichnaya replaced the phrase "Freedom of Religion" with "Freedom of Vodka."

Being second to vodka as the most refined and clarified of distillates, gin is not to be outdone. Some gin ads have advanced with a cleaner, more sparkling and mystical guise. In the case of Bombay's Sapphire Gin, the crystallization comes from adding rather than refining. To its mixture, Bombay's Sapphire supplements at least ten essential botanicals for a fragrance that could very well enhance the sensation of drifting.

This is a stunning example of how the sacred and the profane can merge. The mystical arguments, so foggy and intangible when applied to traditional metaphysics and theology, suddenly become concrete when transubstantiated inside of a long-stemmed chalice.

Ethyl and Ether. The cult of the cocktail offers an upward odyssey complete with ten alcohol emanations. You begin with the densest of elements with such earthy concoctions as wine; rise up to such intermediary distillations as brandy, scotch, or cognac; then soar to reach gin and vodka, the most clarified of the spirits. Through modern marketing, gin can become a molten crystal monitor revealing images of an inner peace to replace the daily grind. Refracted through the stained-glass window of a clean Martini, the world can assume a prismatic purity that is bigger than life and at least equal to God. (© Carillon Importers Ltd., Teaneck, N.J.)

14

*It Was a Very Good
Year Today*

Old soldiers and sailors and airmen don't die. They go to
cocktail parties. And they try to go to another cocktail party.
—Craig Wilson, *USA Today,* reporting on the
celebrity *QE2* cruise to commemorate
D-Day's 50th Anniversary

Each time Frank Sinatra croons "It Was a Very
Good Year," a succession of past, present, and future
lives passes through the listener's mind. Generations
slur into an arabesque of identities and attitudes as the
Ervin M. Drake tune relates a melancholy retrospective
that likens human existence to "vintage wine." With each
raising of the cocktail glass, people toast the past, hoping
they may embrace an eternal family of drinkers who con-
gregate in a vintner's Valhalla.

In 1981, when Nancy Reagan proudly announced
that the White House would serve hard liquor once again,
the eighties had signaled a return to "traditional values"—
not just of the home, dog, white-picket fence, and church
veneer that Ronald Reagan presented to the press, but of

the freewheeling, backroom card-shark ethos of high-toned dining, flashy apparel, and drinks galore. After all, Frank Sinatra (once a bastion of sixties liberalism) had long since turned Republican and was on hand to embrace the Reagans at both inaugural parties.

A change took place in the eighties—a confused decade that makes the seventies seem idyllic by comparison. Old icons were dusted off and rehabilitated into fashion statements. Among the rediscovered artifacts was the classic cocktail, still hurting after years of neglect and misunderstanding. The cocktail reemerged with the same ambiguous associations it had just after Prohibition.

The Reagan White House may have welcomed the cocktail back, but a 1987 trade dispute involving exports of American grain to Europe impelled the President to counter exorbitant grain tariffs with equally high tariffs on such delicacies as gin from Britain and olives from Greece. This sparked what *The New York Times* referred to as the "martini war."

To the White House, Martinis and Highballs may have meant a return to paradise. To an early eighties Dada-inspired rock group calling itself "Drunk Driving," they represented the excesses of fat cats bent on escalating the war between rich and poor. The group's members were known to scrawl graffiti manifestoes along New York's Alphabet City walls in between cacophonous guitar feedback and wailing vocal performances in abandoned warehouses and on street corners. Changing its name to "Missing Foundation," the band's founder, Peter Missing, chose the upside-down cocktail glass as its symbol, signifying their militant credo, "The Party's Over."

However, these incidents had proved to be a tempest brewing out of a, dare we say, teetotaler's pot! With the rapid renovation of cities and a gentrified populace seeking to rediscover America in its proper capitalist image, young people (regardless of their political beliefs) felt more inclined to agree with Nancy Reagan's suggestion that cocktails help make the world a more pleasant place.

There was a gradual but noticeable shift from theaters of political warfare to theaters of leisure. A pining for retro beauty surfaced, capturing yesteryear's ocean-liner elegance. In 1987, the Promenade Bar in New York's Rainbow Room was redesigned, with the Mickey Mouse law of curves as its inspiration. Based on the belief that circles are more soothing and reassuring than angles, the designers avoided jagged edges. They removed the old mirrors and plants to expose the New York skyline, making the Rainbow Room's Promenade Bar a contrast between the dark sky and the indoor lights. According to its designer Hugh Hardy: "The new set-up helps make patrons less self-conscious and more prone to the visceral cues of others. You see the skyline from sixty-five floors. But instead of feeling vulnerable being so far up, the low ceilings and low lighting give a sheltered feeling."

New York's Royalton got a similar multimillion-dollar facelift. French designer Philippe Starck set it in a chromium fin de siècle style that seems both majestic and mildly threatening with its angular contours and surgical steel awnings. Located diagonally across from the Algonquin on West Forty-fourth Street, the Royalton first opened in 1898 and had since become a Manhattan landmark. In 1988, it got the theme-park treatment, presided over by former Studio 54 magnates Ian Schrager (one of the hotel's owners) and Steve Rubell. Both applied the principles of "lounge" to a doctrine they call "hotel as theater," intent on making the Royalton "the hotel of the nineties" by emphasizing the importance of "lobby socializing" and installing a "round bar" inspired by Paris's The Ritz (among Ernest Hemingway's favorite haunts).

The distiller industries, aware of a new market niche on the horizon, started flavoring their gin and vodka ads with various "in" jokes. Tanqueray had introduced "Mr. Jenkins," a character that would soon grace billboards, public transportation stops, and magazine inserts. Mr. Jenkins was the suave, sophisticated gent appointed to lure Generation Xers into a swinger lifestyle that their parents (or more likely grandparents) once revered. Appearing in a variety of situations—from pool halls to posh parties—in which young urban adults often find themselves, he encourages them to accessorize with Martinis, Gimlets, or Gin-and-Tonics.

Thanks to the advertising acumen of Deutsch Inc. and its estimated $27 million publicity launch, Mr. Jenkins may seem just a cut-out head pasted onto various tableaux, but a spirit issues from his half placid, half maniacal expression that evokes country club comportment but also a plucky side which may prefer drag bars over office parties. Who is Mr. Jenkins, really? What does he represent? And why does he promise to exert such a hold on the gin-loving public (for whom Tanqueray boasts a market of at least 60 percent)?

According to his press agents, Mr. Jenkins comes from "somewhere on the planet" and is "tight-lipped about his origins." His was a "privileged and cultured upbringing." With several degrees and an education culled from the classrooms of Harvard, Oxford, West Point, and the University of Tibet, he also had "a brief stint at Hoffenberg Cocktail Mixology Institute, where a monument was built in his honor."

Yet this "official" explanation of Mr. Jenkins makes him even more mysterious. He is a part of a dynasty whose power is ancient yet undying. Though he may be among the economically privileged, his allure affects the tastes and customs of a more modest but no less searching middle class eager for yet more intimations of the "good life."

In 1994, as Mr. Jenkins corralled one generation, the majestic *QE2* took World War II veterans on a celebrity cruise to commemorate D-Day's 50th Anniversary. Over 1,800 sailed on the luxury liner from the British coast to Normandy's beaches. On hand was Bob Hope, squeezing chuckles out of standing-room-only crowds, while songstress Vera Lynn rekindled the hearts of wartime sweethearts once hypnotized by her rendition of "We'll Meet Again." There were also such figures as Walter Cronkite and Edwin Newman, who offered nostalgic talks, while the Glenn Miller Orchestra played "Sentimental Journey," "Night and Day," "(There'll Be Bluebirds Over) The White

Cliffs of Dover," and other standards in the background. Reporting on the event in *USA Today,* journalist Craig Wilson remarked that there were "dry martinis and wet eyes," thanks to 1,000 bottles of champagne, 600 bottles of gin, and 1,500 pounds of lobster.

And what were these revellers' grandchildren up to? They were holding their own cocktail rituals, adopting the poses, musical styles, and drink recipes from bygone eras. At a club in London's Soho district, for instance, patrons could sip drinks while lounging in sixties-style swivel chairs as the easy-listening sounds of Mancini and Mantovani swelled through the atmosphere.

In the States, a Boston rock-and-roll club usually carpeted with cigarette butts and stale beer was transformed into a "Tiki Wonder Hour," refurbished with palm fronds, an Easter Island head, a synthetic volcano, nightclub tables with lanterns, and a totem pole of television sets projecting Sinatra, Dean Martin, Sammy Davis Jr., and other crooners of yesteryear. The Tiki Wonder Hour's star act was Combustible Edison (the name of both a musical ensemble and its promotional cocktail), which played an olio of music for cocktail lounges and spy movies. The event even produced a *First Manifesto of the Cocktail Nation,* which stated: "We, the citizens of the Cocktail Nation, do hereby declare our independence from the desiccated horde of mummified uniformity—our freedom from an existence of abject swinglessness."

That old image of the crooner crying into his drink and waxing misty over a past full of pain and laughter also lives on. Tony Bennett became the first senior citizen to have a hit MTV video while Sinatra performed a series of duets with some rock stars. The unbeatable Sinatra, who ascended from the ashes many times, promises to rise again and again. He may have collapsed during his Richmond performance in 1994, but in memory, he got right back up. Sinatra's fall (even without his drink) suggests how much cocktail culture upholds its own fluid dynamics. Imagine if it were possible to diagram the orbit of all the ritual drinkers who fall off bar stools and continue to rise again. On the surface, the patterns of this pie-eyed pendulum may appear a chaotic mishmash, the mere doodlings of a demented preschooler. But within those seemingly chaotic tangents, we may begin to glean an inner order that might help explain why every other generation produces a fresh breed of cocktail adherents who are not afraid to take the plunge.

It is as if Sinatra's mishap were rectified by a movie camera's saving graces. We can imagine his fall filmed in reverse: Sinatra returns from his downward trajectory back to a vertical dignity, this time with drink in hand, to reassure us there are more very good years ahead, more wee small hours that get stranger in the night . . .

A Cocktail Cleansing. As the champagne bottle whispered "Drink Me," the newlyweds prepared their nuptial bath. They toasted to success, to health, and to eternal romance. The cocktail, far from being just an accoutrement, took its rightful place as a spiritual centerpiece. In *Alice in Wonderland* fashion, the drink expanded to a hundred times its size, enticing the lovers to enter the cauldron of comfort and oblivion. (Caesars Pocono Resorts, located in the Pocono Mountains of Pennsylvania, Patent #DES-294,290)

BIBLIOGRAPHY

ARTICLES

"A Peach of a Drink." *Time*, 24 August 1987, 63.

Abrams, Isabel S. "Beyond Night and Day." *Space World,* vol. W-12-276 (December 1986): 12–13. Charles Winget's work on circadian rhythms and astronauts.

Ceplius, Stan, illus. "Mixing the Perfect Martini." *Playboy,* September 1955, 17+.

Chrysanthe, Eva, illus. "Monkey Bar Reopens," *The New York Observer*, 26 September 1994.

"Cocktail Parties—Are Hosts People?" *Newsweek,* 2 May 1960, 25.

Della Femina, Jerry. "The Heyday of the Three-Martini Lunch," *New York Times Magazine*, 29 October 1989, S-22.

DeVoto, Bernard. "For the Wayward and Beguiled." *Harpers,* December 1949, 68–71.

Dolven, Frank. "The Many Faces of Al Capone." *Big Reel,* November 1994, 137–142.

"Drier & Drier." *Newsweek,* 19 October 1959. Article about the "Dilly-tini" and other attempts to adulterate the classic Martini.

"Drinks' Roots Steeped in History." *Nation's Restaurant News,* 18 September 1989, S-33.

Duffy, Gillian. "Eat, Drink, Be Merry." *New York,* 31 October 1994, 61. Addresses the "postmodern" cocktail.

Dullea, Georgia. "The, Uh, Royalton Round Table." *New York Times,* 27 December 1992.

Elliott, Stuart. "When a stranger offers to buy a drink at the bar, is it flattery, or a walking commercial for Cognac?" *New York Times,* 14 January 1994.

Fisher, M. F. K. "To the Gibson and Beyond." *Atlantic Monthly,* January 1949, 93.

Flanagan, William G. "New York's Friendliest Bars and Bartenders." *Forbes,* 5 December 1994, 282–5.

"Frank Sinatra: A Candid Conversation with the Acknowledged King of Showbiz." *Playboy,* February 1963, 35.

Glenn, Joshua. "Cocktail Nation." *Cake,* vol. 11, no. 22, 1994, 24-33.

Gonzalez, Donald J. "Crisis at the Cocktail Hour." *Saturday Review,* 15 November 1975, 46–48.

Grimes, William. "Through a Cocktail Glass Darkly (Hold the Olive)." *Miami Herald,* 25 August 1991, 3-C.

Heller, Karen. "The Martini is Coming Back; Strong Dry Spell is Over for the Time-Honored, Civilized Cocktail." *Philadelphia Inquirer,* 9 April 1987, E01.

Hill, Corinne M. and David W. Hill. "Influence of Time of Day on Responses to the Profile of Mood States." *Perceptual and Motor Skills* (April 1991): 434.

Hurley, Patrick. "Cuba Si! Papa No!" *Esquire,* June 1991, 62.

Lubow, Arthur. "This Vodka Has Legs," *New Yorker,* 12 September 1994, 62-83.

Mario, Thomas. "The Beauties of the Bubbly." *Playboy,* January 1961, 39.

———. "By Juniper!" *Playboy,* August 1954, 36.

———. "Captivatingly Clear." *Playboy,* May 1969, 133.

———. "The Cocktail Hour." *Playboy,* October 1955, 22.

———. "Cooling It by the Numbers." *Playboy,* August 1969, 98.

———. "Gentleman Julep." *Playboy,* August 1966, 115.

———. "Gin Fling." *Playboy,* May 1964, 82.

———. "Ice & Easy." *Playboy,* August 1967, 102.

———. "Playboy at the Punch Bowl." *Playboy,* February 1955, 16.

———. "Proofs Positive." *Playboy,* May 1965, 94.

———. "Rum Antics." *Playboy,* June 1970, 112.

"Martini Heresy." *Life,* 10 December 1951, 81–82.

Mura, Elaine L., and David A. Levy. "Relationship Between Neuroticism and Circadian Rhythms." *Psychological Reports,* vol. 58 (February 1986): 298.

Perkins, H. Wesley. "Religious Traditions, Parents, and Peers as Determinants of Alcohol and Drug Use Among College Students." *Review of Religious Research,* September 1985, 15–31.

"The *Playboy* Panel: The Womanization of America." *Playboy,* June 1962, 43.

"*Playboy*'s TV Penthouse: The Urban Men's Magazine Brings Its Fun and Sophistication to Television." *Playboy,* March 1960, 41–43

Ponte, Lowell. "The Two Most Dangerous Hours of Your Day." *Reader's Digest,* March 1992, 11–12.

Pope, Jon, and Mike Allen. "Sinatra alert after collapse." *Richmond Times-Dispatch,* 7 March 1994, 1.

Robins, Wayne. "High Spirits: Uptown and Down, Martinis are Back in Style." *New York Newsday,* 29 June 1994, B-27.

"Seventeen Guests and What've You Got?" *Newsweek,* 2 February 1959, 27. Brief overview of Dr. William R. MacLean's study "On the Acoustics of Cocktail Parties."

"Sinatra Faints on Stage." *New York Post,* 7 March 1994, 1, 3.

"Sinatra Stricken." *New York Daily News,* 7 March 1994, 1, 7.

"So Long, Shirley Temple Cocktail: Hello Zinger." *Changing Times,* October 1984, 16.

Storm, Thomas, and R. E. Cutler. "Observations of drinking in natural settings: Vancouver beer parlors and cocktail lounges." *Journal of Studies on Alcohol,* November 1981, vol. 42, 972–97.

Tamony, Peter. "Western Words: Martini Cocktail." *Western Folklore,* April 1967, Berkeley & Los Angeles: University of California Press, 124-7.

Tucker, Chris. "A Generation Fernified." *American Way,* 1 July 1994, 40, 42, 47. A short history of the fern bar.

VanderBeke, Diane M. *The Cocktail Age: 1920s European-Inspired Luxury vs. 1930s Streamlined Based Metals as Evidenced by American Cocktail Shaker Production.* New York: The Cooper-Hewitt Museum and The Parsons School of Design, April 1990.

"When the Bogeyman Clocks On." *The Economist,* 26 November 1988, 94. Overview of Institute of Circadian Physiology (ICP).

Wilson, Craig. "A Cruise of Cocktails and Memories." *USA Today,* 6 June 1994, D1-2. Report on 50th Anniversary of D-Day Celebration on the *QE2.*

Wylie, Philip. "The Womanization of America." *Playboy,* September 1958.

COCKTAIL AND BAR BOOKS

Amis, Kingsley. *On Drink.* New York: Harcourt Brace Jovanovich, Inc., 1970, 1972.

Bergeron, Victor. *Trader Vic's Bartender's Guide, Revised.* Garden City, New York: Doubleday & Company, Inc., 1947, 1972.

Byron, O. H. *The Modern Bartender's Guide.* New York, 1884.

Conrad, Barnaby, III. *The Martini.* San Francisco: Chronicle Books, 1995.

Craddock, Harry. *The Savoy Cocktail Book.* London: Constable & Company, Ltd., 1930.

Crocket, A. S. *The Old Waldorf-Astoria Bar Book.* New York: Dodd, Mead and Co., 1934.

DeVoto, Bernard. *The Hour.* 1948. Reprint, Cambridge, Mass.: The Riverside Press, 1951.

Edmunds, Lowell. *The Silver Bullet: The Martini in American Civilization.* Westport, Conn.: Greenwood Press, 1981.

Foley, Ray. *The Ultimate Cocktail Book.* Livingston, New Jersey: Foley Publishing, 1990.

Grimes, William. *Straight Up or On the Rocks: A Cultural History of American Drink.* New York: Simon & Schuster, 1993.

Lolli, Giorgio. *Social Drinking: How to Enjoy Drinking Without Being Hurt by It.* Cleveland and New York: The World Publishing Co., 1960.

McDonough, P. *McDonough's Bar-keeper's Guide.* Rochester, N.Y., 1883.

Mr. Boston Official Bartender's and Party Guide. New York: Warner Books, 1994.

Oudtshoorn, Nic Van. *The Hangover Handbook.* Memphis, Tenn.: Mustang Publishing Co., 1993.

Spalding, Jill. *Blithe Spirits: A Toast to the Cocktail.* Washington, D.C.: Alvin Rosenbaum Projects, Inc., 1988.

Thomas, Jerry. *How to Mix Drinks or The Bon Vivant's Companion,* New York, 1862.

OTHER BOOKS

Aries, Philippe, and Georges Duby, eds. *A History of Private Life: From the Fires of Revolution to the Great War.* Trans. Arthur Goldhammer. Cambridge, Mass.: The Belknap Press of Harvard University Press, 1990. Discusses the role of the traditional alehouse and public drinking.

Ballard, J. G. *The Terminal Beach.* Middlesex, England: Penguin Books, 1964.

Barnes, Hazel Estella. *The Meddling Gods: Four Essays on Classical Themes.* Lincoln, Nebr.: University of Nebraska Press, 1974. Probes Eliot's *The Cocktail Party*'s references to ancient mythology and modern existentialism.

Cavendish, Richard. *The Black Arts*. New York: A Wideview/ Perigee Book, 1967. Briefly discusses alcohol's occult significance.

Chandler, Raymond. *The Long Goodbye*. New York: Vintage Books, 1981.

Cheever, John. *The Short Stories of John Cheever*. New York: Ballantine Books, 1978. Provides some priceless cocktail culture character sources.

Clarke, Gerald. *Capote: A Biography*. New York: Simon & Schuster, 1988.

Corn, Joseph J., and Brian Horrigan. *Yesterday's Tomorrows*. New York: Summit Books, 1984.

Coslow, Sam. *Cocktails for Two*. New Rochelle, New York: Arlington House, 1977.

Dardis, Tom. *The Thirsty Muse: Alcohol and the American Writer*. New York: Ticknor & Fields, 1989.

Davis, Mike. *City of Quartz*. New York: Vintage Books, 1990.

Davis, Sammy, Jr., and Jane & Burt Boyer. *Yes I Can: The Story of Sammy Davis, Jr.* New York: Farrar, Straus & Giroux, 1965.

Eliot, T. S. *The Cocktail Party*. New York: A Harvest/HBJ Book, 1950, 1978.

Freidel, Frank. *Franklin D. Roosevelt: A Rendezvous with Destiny*. Boston: Little, Brown and Company, 1990.

Gabler, Neal. *Winchell: Gossip, Power and the Culture of Celebrity*. New York: Alfred A. Knopf, 1994.

Goldstein, Malcolm. *George S. Kaufman: His Life, His Theater*. New York: Oxford University Press, 1979.

Gould, Heywood. *Cocktail*. New York: St. Martin's Press, 1984.

Hecht, Anthony. *Millions of Strange Shadows*. New York: Athaeneum, 1977.

Hemingway, Ernest. *Across the River and into the Trees*. New York: Charles Schribner's Sons, 1950.

———. *A Farewell to Arms*. New York: Charles Scribner's Sons,

———. *The Sun Also Rises*. 1926. Reprint, New York: Charles Scribner's Sons, 1954.

Hoffman, Frederick J. *The Twenties: American Writing in the Postwar Decade*. New York: Collier Books, 1962.

Hofstadter, Richard. *The Age of Reform*. New York: Vintage Books, 1955.

Johnson, Diane. *Dashiell Hammett: A Life*. New York: Fawcett Columbine, 1985.

Kelley, Kitty. *His Way: The Unauthorized Biography of Frank Sinatra.* New York: Bantam Books, 1986.

Key, Wilson Bryan. *Subliminal Seduction.* New York: A Signet Book, 1973.

Krutnik, Frank. *In a Lonely Street: Film noir, genre, masculinity.* London and New York: Routledge, 1993.

LaVey, Anton Szandor. *The Devil's Notebook.* Portland, Oreg: Feral House, 1992.

Lee, Henry. *How Dry We Were: Prohibition Revisited.* Englewood Cliffs, New Jersey: Prentice-Hall, Inc., 1963.

Leff, Leonard J., and Jerold L. Simmons. *The Dame in the Kimono: Hollywood, Censorship, and the Production Code from the 1920s to the 1960s.* New York: Grove Weidenfeld, 1990.

Levin, Ira. *Rosemary's Baby.* New York: Random House, 1967.

Lockley, Ronald M. *Animal Navigation.* New York: Hart Publishing Company, Inc., 1967.

London, Jack. *Burning Daylight.* New York: Macmillan, 1910.

––––––. *John Barleycorn; or, Alcoholic Memoirs.* 1913, Reprint, New York: A Signet Classic, 1990.

Lynch, Kevin. *What Time Is This Place?* Cambridge, Mass.: The MIT Press, 1993.

Morris, Desmond. *The Human Zoo.* New York: McGraw-Hill, 1969.

Niven, David. *Bring On the Empty Horses.* New York: G. P. Putnam's Sons, 1975.

Passos, John Dos. *Manhattan Transfer.* 1925. Reprint, Boston: Houghton Mifflin, 1953.

Post, Elizabeth L. *Emily Post's Etiquette.* 15th ed. New York: Harper Collins Publishers, 1992.

Reisman, David (with Nathan Glazer and Reuel Denney). *The Lonely Crowd: A Study of the Changing American Character.* Garden City, N.Y.: Doubleday Anchor Books, 1950, 1953.

Rodgers, Marion Elizabeth, ed. *The Impossible H.L. Mencken.* New York: Doubleday, 1991.

Schivelbusch, Wolfgang. *Tastes of Paradise: A Social History of Spices, Stimulants, and Intoxicants.* New York: Pantheon Books, 1992.

Schneider, Charles, ed. *CAD: A Handbook for Heels.* Los Angeles: Feral House, Inc., 1972.

Schulberg, Budd. *What Makes Sammy Run?* Cambridge, Mass.: Robert Bentley, 1979.

Schwartz, Charles. *Cole Porter: A Biography.* New York: The Dial Press, 1977.

Shea, Robert, and Robert Anton Wilson. *Illuminatus!* New York: A Dell Trade Paperback, 1975.

Shepherd, Donald, and Robert F. Slatzer. *Bing Crosby: The Hollow Man.* New York: St. Martin's Press, 1981.

Sinclair, Upton. *The Wet Parade.* London: T. Werner Laurie Ltd., 1931.

Smith, Carol H. *T. S. Eliot's Dramatic Theory and Practice: From Sweeney Agonistes to the Elder Statesman.* Princeton, New Jersey: Princeton University Press, 1963.

Spillane, Mickey. *Vengeance Is Mine.* New York: A Signet Book, 1951.

Symons, Julian. *Dashiell Hammett.* New York: Harcourt Brace Jovanovich, 1985.

Tiger, Lionel. *Men in Groups.* New York: Random House, 1969.

Tinbergen, Niko. *The Animal in Its World.* Cambridge, Mass.: Harvard University Press, 1973.

Tosches, Nick. *Dino.* New York: A Dell Book, 1992.

Venturi, Robert, Denise Scott Brown, and Steven Izenour. *Learning from Las Vegas.* Revised ed. Cambridge, Mass.: The MIT Press, 1993.

Whyte, William H., Jr. *The Organization Man.* New York: A Touchstone Book, 1956.

Wilder, Thornton. *Our Town.* 1938. Reprint, New York: Perennial Library, 1985.

Williams, Tennessee. *The Roman Spring of Mrs. Stone.* 1950, Reprint, New York: New Directions, 1993.

Wilson, Earl. *Sinatra: An Unauthorized Biography.* New York: Macmillan Publishing Co., Inc., 1976.

Wilson, Sloan. *The Man in the Gray Flannel Suit.* Thorndike, Maine: Thorndike Press, 1955.

Wodehouse, P. G. *Cocktail Time.* 1958. Reprint, London: Penguin Books, 1987.

Wylie, Philip. *Opus 21.* New York: Pocket Books, Inc., 1950.

INDEX